HOW SAFE IS OUR INVESTMENT

HOW SAFE IS OUR INVESTMENT

Rethinking a Pathway for a Dynamic Economic Environment

PAUL OKOYE

AuthorHouse™ UK Ltd.
1663 Liberty Drive
Bloomington, IN 47403 USA
www.authorhouse.co.uk
Phone: 0800.197.4150

© 2014 Paul Okoye. All rights reserved.

No part of this book may be reproduced, stored in a retrieval system, or transmitted by any means without the written permission of the author.

Published by AuthorHouse   10/13/2014

ISBN: 978-1-4969-8879-9 (sc)
ISBN: 978-1-4969-8878-2 (hc)
ISBN: 978-1-4969-8880-5 (e)

Any people depicted in stock imagery provided by Thinkstock are models, and such images are being used for illustrative purposes only. Certain stock imagery © Thinkstock.

This book is printed on acid-free paper.

Because of the dynamic nature of the Internet, any web addresses or links contained in this book may have changed since publication and may no longer be valid. The views expressed in this work are solely those of the author and do not necessarily reflect the views of the publisher, and the publisher hereby disclaims any responsibility for them.

CONTENTS

Abstract vii
Context ix
Introduction xi
Foreword xiii

Chapter 1 Hypotheses, Theories, and Explanations
 of Investments 1
Chapter 2 Causes of the Crisis 5
Chapter 3 Effects of the Crisis 18
Chapter 4 Economic Implications of the Failed Investment 25
Chapter 5 Social Implications of the Failed Investment 34
Chapter 6 Legal Implications of Failed Investments 43
Chapter 7 Democratic Impediment and Political
 Implications of the Failed Investment 51

Afterword 77
Glossary 81
Bibliography 85

ABSTRACT

After an extensive study and review of relevant factors affecting investment, *How Safe Is Our Investment?* is centred on the failure of investments. But since investment does not exist in isolation, the aim therefore is to understand exactly why investments fail in relation to political, social, and economic constraints.

The simultaneous failure of various investments leads to financial crises, and financial crises trigger economic crises because of the interrelationship between investment and the economy. It is a generally accepted belief that investment goes with risk. Investment theory also holds this position. This book is not concerned with the natural forces or phenomena that affect investments and often leads to the failure of investment. By natural factor, I mean the traditional environment under which investments exist. This could be market conditions or microeconomic and macroeconomic factors. The aim of this book is to explore the dimension of human factor to investment failure with special attention to the current economic crisis. The dimension of human nature we are mostly concerned with is the egoistic nature. How does man contribute to the destruction of economic investment in the propagation of his interest?

I also analysed the consequences of failed investments from a political, social, legal, and economic point of view. Part of the economic consequences of failed investment is that it leads to loss of capital as well as property. The loss of capital leads to the lack of essential capacity for future investment, triggering further problems in the future, especially retardation or lack of growth. The result is a decrease in aggregate demand and supply with a direct effect on GDP (gross domestic product).

After a critical analysis of the environment surrounding investments, *How Safe Is Our Investment?* explains that although investment is associated with risk, most times the circumstances that lead to the failure of investments are traceable to other factors. These factors could be wrong application of macroeconomics or accounting principles, technological revolution or loose financial policies ("soft law"). Evidently, part of the fallout of the current crisis is that it exposed the weaknesses of most countries and their lack of adoption or wrong application of macroeconomic principles. Sometimes the fear of losing votes induces policymakers to avoid hard decisions. Blanchard[1] said in his book Macroeconomics "many macroeconomic measures involve trading off short-run losses against long-run gains – or, symmetrically, short-run gains against long-run losses" Blanchard (2000, 491).

How Safe Is Our Investment? suggests the way forward as implementing effective laws to help reduce the failure of investment and return the economy to the path of growth.

---

[1] Olivier Blanchard the chief economist of IMF is a professor of economics at Massachusetts Institute of Technology

CONTEXT

Investment is the driver of every economy; therefore, the role of investment in every economy deserves attention. The rapid growth of investments in the past decades has been instrumental in driving the global economic growth. Investment plays an important role in the determination of the wealth of every nation. Of significant importance is the increasing role of emerging markets, which have undoubtedly brought serious changes in the paradigm of investment. This has brought remarkable shifts in the organization and structure of global production. The change has also affected the type of services and products traded. The tradability of services is highly increasing while numerous products like commodities and derivatives are increasingly acquiring large shares in the market.

The shift and readjustment in investment is clearly reshaping the global economy. It is evident that the nature of this change in investment plays a vital role in the determination of the major players in the world economy. The majority of trade and investments initially remained with developed countries, but due to the realignment, things are gradually changing. It is therefore becoming increasingly important to understand the reason for these changes and the dimension investment is taking, especially in the light of the current global financial crisis that has triggered a check in the growth of investment.

Despite the fact that the financial crisis has severe consequences on investments, the fear is that it still holds significant risk for future investment prospects. Policy barriers have affected the attraction of investments in many countries because investors need good economic fundamentals in which to invest, such as market size and growth; good quality and appropriate skill and infrastructure; and local technological capabilities including good policies. Political and economic stability is another important factor in the choice of where to invest. Cost of labour has recently helped in reshaping investment locations. This book examines these trends in relation to investment failures.

INTRODUCTION

How Safe Is Our Investment? has set out to prove that there are factors that play a pivotal role in the decision to invest. These factors also affect the success and failure of investments. The factors are numerous, and each affects investment from a different dimension.

Recent studies have introduced an element of uncertainty to investment theory due to irreversible investment. This has brought another view to the factors that influence the success and failure of investments. The position of *How Safe Is Our Investment?* is that investment is the nucleus of an economy, and it plays a crucial role in the models of economic growth. Let me also add that it is an essential component of aggregate demand, and fluctuations in investments have considerable effect on economic activity and long-term economic growth.

'Tobin's Q' theory[2], or ratio, of investment as elaborated by William C. Brainard and James Tobin (1977) made a significant contribution to the study of investment behaviour when it said that "the ratio of the market value of the existing capital stock to its replacement cost (the Q ratio) is the main force driving investment." The emphasis is that there is a direct correlation between investment and the economy. Therefore the factors that influence the economy directly or indirectly affect investment, which is an integral part of the market. This forms the basis of our arguments in later chapters establishing the human factors that have contributed to investments failures.

---

[2] Tobin's Q theory is an economic theory of investment introduced by WillianC. Brainard and James Tobin in 1968. However the use of the letter "q" did not appear until Tobin's 1969 article "A general equilibrium approach to monetary theory". James Tobin of Yale University, Nobel laureate in economics, hypothesized that the combined market value of all the companies on the stock market should be about equal to their replacement costs.

This points to the economic relation of investment and the economy. Despite economic variables, there are other factors that affect investments. This is because investment decisions and implementations are executed by people, and this brings another dimension to the study of investment. These factors, both economic and human, directly and indirectly affect investment. The failure of investments therefore can be traceable to accounting, political or economic factors.

The failure of investment has serious effects on investors, the economy, and society. The aim of *How Safe Is Our Investment?* is to examine the factors that influence the success and failure of investments with specific attention to their effects in relation to the current financial crisis.

FOREWORD

It is a generally accepted economic principle that business is often a risk. Usually, after every great economic boom follows an economic retardation, argued Olivier Blanchard. This statement supports the fact that investment is associated with risk. However, this work has tried to explain that most business do not fail because of the natural risk and uncertainty associated with investment. Blanchard also made a case in support of this argument in his work when he said, "We have assumed so far that policymakers were benevolent – they tried to do what is best for the economy. However, much public discussions challenge that assumption. Politicians or policymakers, the argument goes, do what is best for themselves, and this is not always what is best for the country. ... Politicians avoid hard decisions; they ponder to the electorate; partisan politics leads to gridlock; and nothing ever gets done" (Blanchard 2000, 491–3).

The statement above reaffirms as I will explain later the fact that policymakers who are politicians – or worse, still appointed by them – usually do not apply the appropriate macroeconomic rules because they do not want to lose votes. The lack of adoption of appropriate economic policy, and measures lead to economic crises that inevitably transform into investment failure.

Lack of effective management also leads to the failure of investments. Daft made a valuable inroad into this position in his work. The success of every business partly depends on good management. Therefore, the lack of effective management hurts the business and leads to the failure of investments (Daft 1994). Accounting principles[3] and regulations have been

---

[3] Accounting principle refer to the fundamental rules or propositions that serves as a foundation in the dispensation and proper functioning of the accounting profession

violated or manipulated to aid fraud in some organizations. This also has led to investment failure.

The case of Parmalat scandal explains how accounting principles can be manipulated to aid fraud by those who run the organization. This book, in looking at the unavoidable risks and uncertainties that lead to investment failure, tries to explain the fact that not all investments fail from the risk associated with it; sometimes there are outside factors. The work also examined investment failure and the hardship and economic realignment that comes with it.

Going forward, if things are done properly by the policymakers, with the right regulations in place, and appropriate and prompt punishment for defaulters, the failure of investments will drastically reduce.

CHAPTER 1

Hypotheses, Theories, and Explanations of Investments

Introduction

After extensive consideration, study, and analysis of relevant information, the potential value of this book could be to contribute to the body of knowledge on the factors affecting investment. This is done by evaluating the potential causes of investment failure, with special attention to current financial and economic crises. *How Safe Is Our Investment?* is relevant and timely because, although literature exists in the area of investment, most take a global view of economy or crisis in relation to investment. This book attempts to synthetically study investment and the factors surrounding its failure. The following is the result of the attempt to establish these factors.

Investment and Factors

Here we will cover the explanation of investment and the factors that positively or negatively influence investment directly or indirectly.

Investment can be defined as the commitment of money or capital into something with the expectation of interest. (The word 'something' suggests investment could be in the form of financial instruments, assets, or trade with the single aim of the appreciation of whatever that is committed into the venture.) Investment is the use of money in the hope of making more money.

There is commitment with expectation, but no certainty of future positive returns, interest, or dividends, so every investment involves a degree of risk. The aim of most study and theory is to reduce or eliminate the risk involved in investment and the decision to invest.

Among these theories of investment is Irving Fisher's theory, which says capital investment is chosen to maximise utility over time (Fisher 1906). John Maynard Keynes's[4] theory on investment proposed that firms are assumed to rank their investment project based on the internal rate of returns (Keynes 1936). The emphasis is that, firms should choose those investments which their internal rate of return exceeds the rate of interest. Financial theory on investment proposes portfolio diversification to reduce investment risk. In principle, financial theory emphasises that the higher the risk, the higher the return and vice versa. Therefore, investors that aspire to higher returns must go for high-risks in their portfolio.

Although these theories made a degree of headway into the study of investments, their shortcomings is that they presume humans that are directly responsible for the application of these theories and the management of investments and organizations are static. The reverse is the case because humans (the most important asset in every organization) are dynamic in nature and therefore have different mindsets, orientations, cultures, perceptions, aspirations, and opinions. What works in organization 'A' may not work in organization 'B' because people in organization A may, for example, employ more corrupt people than those in organization B. Also, the reason for different outcomes could as well be that some organizations are more pressed financially. It could also be based on the greed of the people running the organization, as this book will establish later. The investment and organizational environment is too complex to have a standard rule applicable to all situations.

---

[4] **John Maynard Keynes,** (5 June 1883 – 21 April 1946) was a British economist whose ideas have fundamentally influenced and dominated the theory and practice of modern macroeconomics and informed the economic policies of most governments. He built on and greatly refined previous work on the causes of business cycles, and he is generally considered to be one of the founders of modern macroeconomics and the most prominent and influential economist of the 20th century.

Political Theory

One of the most instrumental factors that determine the success or failure of an investment is the political system of a state. This factor also influences to a great extent the initial investment decision of the private, public, and institutional investors: where to invest and what to invest in. This is because political systems define the economic as well as legal systems of that nation.

There exists two predominant political systems, collectivism and individualism. Collectivism dates back to 427 BC, during the days of the Greek philosopher Plato. Collectivism as a political system stresses the primacy of collective interest over individual interest. This implies that the general need of society supersedes individual interest or freedom.

Individualism refers to the political philosophy that an individual should have freedom in his or her economic and political endeavours. Unlike collectivism, individualism stresses that the interest of an individual will take precedence over the interest of the society, even in reaping the gains and dividends of the investment.

Like collectivism, individualism can also be traced to a Greek philosopher, Aristotle. The logic of this argument is that collectivism gave birth to totalitarianism, the origin of socialism and communism, which stresses protectionism. On the other hand, individualism transformed into democracy, which gave birth to capitalism, the direct offshoot of the free market. Investment nonetheless is attracted more to capitalist economy than command economy, except in rare occasions, such as in China.

Capitalism and Socialism

Proponents of a capitalist economy urge for a level playing ground for all players. Investment performs better in a capitalist society as it emphasises a winner-takes-all mentality. Capitalism leads to economic growth because it encourages innovation and investment. It is a generally accepted argument that innovation and entrepreneurial activity is the engine of long-term economic growth. This is because entrepreneurs are more motivated in a free-market economy. More often than not, investment is the product of entrepreneurial activity through the commercialisation of new products, and entrepreneurs provide much-needed dynamism in an economy. If a country's economy is to sustain long-term economic growth, the business environment must be conducive to investment activity.

It would not be wrong to conclude that investment activity strives better in a free-market economy. The determinant factors are supply and demand effect. This creates a greater incentive for the emergence of entrepreneurial activities, unlike the planned economy where the state owns all means of production. In a planned economy, entrepreneurs have less economic incentives to develop valuable innovations, apparently because it is the state, rather than the individual, that inherits most of the gains (Hill 2009).

Keynes Theory

John Maynard Keynes said, "Apart from the necessity of central controls to bring about an adjustment between the propensity to consume and the inducement to invest, there is no more reason to socialise economic life than there was before" (1936). The theories and works of this British economist John Maynard Keynes have greatly influenced the modern-day macroeconomic principle as well as government economic policies. Keynes advocated the use of fiscal and monetary policies by government to correct the adverse effects of economic depression and recession. In principle, he proposed that government should step in to stimulate economy in the absence of private spending to avoid recession. Government intervention to stimulate the economy, according to Keynes, could be in the form of fiscal or monetary policy as well as government spending. The idea is to keep aggregate demand high and unemployment in check.

But Keynes ideas have been flagrantly abused. The next chapter will explore how this has happened.

CHAPTER 2

Causes of the Crisis

Overspending Policy

In the wrong application of Keynes's theory, the United States, in addition to most Western countries, have been spending more than they earn for many decades, and this partly led to the crisis and consequent investment failure. The internal budget deficit of the United States has remained high for several years. Despite the fact that the European Union's (EU) fiscal regulation fixed the maximum deficit level for individual member nations at 3 per cent, most EU members have constantly violated this rule with impunity.

According to the US treasury department, the deficit for 2009, closing 30 September, was a record $1.42 trillion, while the outstanding national debt was a total of $14.2 trillion as of 25 May 2011. Although the budget deficit figure for the 2010 fiscal year ending 30 September was slightly below the 2009 figure, the amount was a whooping $1.19 trillion. (The budget deficit for Italy's 2010 fiscal year stood at 5.3 per cent of GDP while the national debt is $1.89 trillion, according to the Italian stock exchange.) The United Kingdom's situation is not different, from the US or Italian counterpart, although it rescued three banks. The budget deficit of Britain for the 2010 fiscal year was 12.6 per cent of the GDP, or about £176 billion. This is the highest deficit figure among the twenty-seven-member EU; the debt figure of Britain for 2011 is estimated to be £1.1 trillion. Although many other countries in Africa, South America, and Asia suffer deficits, their situation is more related to fraud than wrong applications of macroeconomic principles.

The figures above go a long way to reinforce the fact that most Western countries have been living above their income for many years. The people who run the economy can not stop spending money they do not have and cannot earn. Every year these countries run large budget deficits, spending more money than they can tax their citizens.

Greg Mankiw maintained that to fill this gap, some of the governments resort to selling bonds at home and internationally. An example is in the United Kingdom, where this type of bond is known as gilt. The problem is that these bonds have to be paid even with interest on maturity. Therefore it's simply an extension of 'doomsday' because everything added together leads to an increment of the national debt. Also, most Western governments, especially the United States', had maintained an adverse balance of trade payment with many countries such as China, India, and Japan. At the end of fiscal year 2010, the United States' exports to China stood at 91.9 billion, while imports from China totalled $364.9 billion, with a total negative trade balance of $273.1 billion. According to US Census Bureau (2011), at the end of January 2011, the trade deficit was a negative figure of $23.3 billion as exports totalled $8.1 billion while imports were $31.3 billion from China alone. Although the trade figures for other countries mentioned above are relatively lower than that of China, they are, however, negative.

This spectacular approach to spending has greatly improved the GDP of the United States and encouraged households to live and spend above their means. About 70 per cent of the US's GDP is composed of household expenditures. After the demise of the gold standard era, the dollar has emerged as the leading reserve currency, and this has helped the US government buy goods and services all over the world and easily make payments using the green paper called the dollar. *The underlying argument is that this habit of the United States government is tantamount to a simple printing of new dollar bills without regard to the real economy.* This act has enabled US citizens to spend above their earnings, thereby living above their capacity and income. The 'Greenspan Put[5]' also encouraged this habit of living above one's means.

The credit card era has not helped matters either. Credit cards have made it possible for people to buy goods and services without money in their pocket or bank account. This has made it possible for credit card holders to recycle their debts. Banks issue loans with minimal or no collateral.

All these go a long way toward reinforcing the spending tendencies or habits of living above one's income.

The Technological Revolution

In relation to the motive of this book, the technological revolution has not helped the situation either, although everything has its merits and demerits. This is because nations like India, china, and other Asian countries can produce goods and services at reduced costs. The consequences of this is that most goods and services, especially finished goods, which used to be the exclusive reserve of the Western nations can now be imported from these nations. The level of the Technological Revolution in these countries is comparable in impact on the world economy with what happened during the Industrial Revolution in Britain beginning in 1760.

In what the author of this work considers a determined application of Smith's principle of the mercantile system, the Chinese have continued to sell goods and services to all customers on relatively low prices and cheap manufacturing costs. In line with the Chinese policy and in the realisation of the mercantile system (zero-sum game) China authorities have decided to keep the value of the RMB down against the US dollar. For the United

---

[5] **The Greenspan Put** refers to the monetary policy approach that Alan Greenspan, the former chairman of the United States Federal Reserve Board, and other Fed members exercised from late 1987 to 2000. The term 'Put' refers to a put option, in which the buyer of the put acquires the right to sell an asset at a particular price to a counterparty; it can be exercised if prices decline below that price. http://en.wikipedia.org/wiki/Greenspan_put

States and other Western consumers, it has been possible to purchase goods and services at unimaginable prices, at least in the past decade. However, this has directly or indirectly led to the crisis as it encouraged the tendency to spend more than the consumer could afford.

Collateralized Debt Obligation

Experience has shown in the recent past that due to developments in the financial sector, economies may be more exposed to financial sector-induced turmoil than in the past. In the United States, the overspending habit encouraged the excessive use of certain financial operations, like the collateralized debt obligation (CDO). The CDO multiplied the effect of the housing bubble burst (subprime crisis), which was the immediate cause of the financial shakeup that triggered the failure of investments.

The CDO is a collection of different types of credit and risk, often referred to as slices or tranches. CDO security is uniquely structured in a way where each slice has a different date of maturity and risk. The higher rate the CDO pays, the higher the risk. This is because the CDO is divided into different risk tranches, whereby senior tranches are considered more secure than junior tranches. Although the CDOs do not specialize in one type of debt, they are often bonds, non-mortgage loans, or assets backed by security. The CDO made an inroad into the financial market in 1987, but remained relatively unknown until 2004. However, between 2004 and 2007, the CDO reached its peak of usefulness as a tool in the hands of financial operators to readily exploit the system. The word subprime qualifies the credit status of the borrower, while subprime lending refers to any loan that does not meet the standard guidelines.

Subprime Lending

The subprime crisis is the direct consequence of subprime lending. In financial circles, subprime lending, which is sometimes called near prime or second-chance lending, refers to the lending of money to customers who do not meet the standard requirements for lending. It means people that fall within this category may have difficulty repaying the borrowed money, and as a result may not have access to borrowing in the credit market in the future. The lack of access to credit is usually related to the credit rating of the borrowers, which entail the record of their borrowing, earning, and lending history. Sometimes it could be caused by a lack of assets or collaterals. A subprime loan is riskier because of the degree of default and therefore carries a higher interest rate.

The Subprime Crisis

Banks and financial institutions usually refuse to lend money to those who have no income or poor credit history. However, in the early 2000s, the global economy was booming and there was excess capital globally. This aided a large influx of capital into the US economy from many parts of the world, especially the emerging nations like oil-producing countries, Asia, and African nations. The huge flow of capital into the US economy, coupled with low interest rates, encouraged easy lending conditions that boasted housing and credit bubbles but set the conditions for the present crisis.

During that period, it was unimaginable to think of the current global financial crises. The only concern of the financial managers was where to invest the capital to yield the highest return; there existed a financial malady, and the name was 'greed'. The concept was that *excess capital must go somewhere*. Generally, in the financial circle low-risk investments yield low returns, and high-risk investments yield high returns. Therefore, since there were no low-risk investments with high returns, the alternative was a shift of high capital to the US mortgage market.

Most of these capital transfers to the mortgage market happened through securitization. Again, debts were recirculated and sold. When a customer obtains a loan from a broker, the broker sells the loan to the bank, which in return sells the loan to an investment firm on Wall Street. The investment firm will collect these pile of loans and sell them back to investors, who are ready to buy to keep or resell. It was a vicious cycle.

These loans were initially backed with collateral, and investors loved it. The financial market was booming and yearning for more. At this point, everybody who needed a loan usually got it. The banks really did not worry about these loans because they were not keeping them but selling them to Wall Street, and Wall Street sold them to global investors. Investors continued to invest based on the advice of the credit-rating agencies like Standard & Poor's, Moody's, and Fitch. The rating agencies continued to rate these investments high, especially as the rate of defaults were low. As the supply pressure remained high, loan seekers did not have to prove anything. All that was required to secure a loan or mortgage was a credit score. This habit of the high-risk loan extended to almost every part of the globe.

The Subprime Mortgage Crisis

The difficulty of securing a loan at a point became a thing of the past because to secure a loan, a customer needed a simple credit score. Since it was so easy to secure a loan, more people wanted to buy a house.

The economic incentives that accrued to the lenders including outright fraud increased the amount of loan available to borrowers in the market. The demand for houses pushed the prices higher, and the high prices attracted more investors, who invested in building more houses for sale. Other investors bought houses to sell at yet a higher rate in the future.

As the prices of house continued to soar, those who could not afford to pay their mortgage simply rescheduled the loan. Others took a second loan at the current rate on the house on the notion that the price of their house had appreciated, in order to refinance the previous loan. This increased the debt burden and the overspending habits of the customers, which finally led to the market turmoil and financial crisis that led to investment failure.

Household income remained constant while the price of houses continued to rise, until it reached the saturation point. Houses became unaffordable, debtors began to default, and refinancing became costly as interest rates appreciated, therefore diminishing return set in. The defaulters put more houses in the already-saturated market, and house prices began to drop. The subsequent rise in interest rates enabled the decline in the price of houses. This continued until the price of houses reached the lowest level in late 2006 and early 2007, and panic set in on Wall Street. The Wall Street investor refused to buy risky loans, and some of the financial investors that sold risky loans started losing their market, with the inevitable consequence of going out of business or job termination.

At this point, no financial or macroeconomic measure could save the world of the impending financial disaster. Worse still, the financial authorities and the Federal Reserve considered the phenomenon an isolated one, and no measure was taken to address the lingering crises until the burble burst. Apparently they did not realise the importance and increasing role of certain financial institutions, such as investment banks and hedge funds. Although these financial institutions had grown almost to equal proportion in the services of lending and providing credit to the US economy, they were still not subject to the same regulations. The implication is that most of these institutions, including the regulated banks, after absorbing these loans do not have the financial cushion to fall back in time of default. If the had it was not enough. Already the financial market had assimilated so much of these risky loans; therefore the bubble would definitely burst.

These 'AAA–rated' loans had already been bought by numerous investors – individuals and financial institutions alike from around the world. What was previously not known to these investors because of the complex nature of the loans came to light, and it became clear that theses loans were worth less than half their initial value. Consequently, investments failed, and investors lost huge amounts of money. A financial crisis had begun and a catastrophic one as events evolved. The financial crisis, due to its complexity, did not help matters as issues pertaining to foreclosures were close to impossible to resolve. Because these loans had been sold, resold, and recycled, piled into securities, and sold to investors, it was difficult if not impossible to trace who the original owners were.

Towards the end of 2010, about 23 per cent of US homes were worth less than the price of the initial mortgage loan. Although this provided a financial incentive for lenders to seek reacquisition of their property by means of foreclosure, it also provided an incentive for debtors to default because it had become cheaper to buy new homes than to finance previous ones.

The investment failure and consequent loss of capital in the subprime market triggered turbulence in the global financial system. Technological advancements in communications have already reduced the world to a global village. Therefore, the subprime crisis spread to the global financial institutions with amazing speed.

Records showed that speculation usually had a big impact on the financial market. Therefore, even markets and other financial institutions with no access to subprime mortgage lending were affected because of the inter-connectedness of the financial system. This caused the loss of confidence among financial institutions. The stock market was systematically weakened. The share prices of all investment banks, large and small, drastically reduced. Between late 2007 and early 2008, most of these banks had already lost almost a third of their value. Banks finally developed cold feet towards each other as trust was lost, leading to a disruption in interbank lending globally. In March 2008 Bear Stearns Companies went off market, while in July, Indy Mac Services degenerated into receivership. September witnessed the financial earthquake, which was the crashing of Lehman Brothers. The financial crisis had gone out of control and escalated to other markets including the mainstream. Overspending clearly contributed to the cause of the present crisis that led to the failure of investments.

Macroeconomic Policies and Investments

Bearing in mind that the aim of this book is to explore the effects of failed investments, it is still important to understand why investments fail, as stated in the previous chapter. I will further address this issue from a macroeconomic viewpoint.

It is clearly evident that macroeconomic situations play a pivotal role in investment decisions, performance, and appraisal. Factors such as interest rate, inflation, GDP, price index, and earning directly affect business investments, while profitability could be hindered by such factors as aggregate income, inflation rate, and unemployment. The cost of capital is influenced by interest rates and exchange rates. The fiscal and monetary policies, like monetary contraction and expansion, of the government and central banks tend to control or direct the economy, and therefore investments, as we shall see later.

The regulation of monetary supply is a powerful tool in the hands of the central bank to control inflation and economic growth. These tools are interrelated and are sometimes used as corrective measures to combat or regulate each other. How does this happen? I will answer that question in the following chapters.

Countries suffering inflation or deficit may need to adopt monetary contraction (the monetary policy that reduces the size of the money circulated in an economy) or tax increases as corrective measures. Inflation is a monetary function; therefore continued monetary contraction may lead to deflation and failure or lack of investment in the longer run. Lack of investment leads to unemployment as well unemployment has adverse effect on investment. A country that embarks on monetary contraction may need to lower the interest rate to stimulate investment and combat unemployment. Every macroeconomic measure has positive and adverse effects and these trade-offs has to be adjusted in the long run.

Because inflation is a monetary function, investments seek to maximise real return over inflation. Inflation reduces the purchasing power of money and can lead to higher demand in wages and unemployment. Inflation leads to uncertainty in the future, thereby making planning difficult. Hurdle rates (the rate of return that a fund manager must beat before collecting incentive fees) can lead to the cancellation of investments and projects, which can lead to low capital investment that may destroy long-run economic growth and productivity. Cost-push inflation (a type of inflation caused by substantial increases in the cost of important goods or services where no suitable alternative is available) can reduce company profit.

The fluctuation of interest rates affects investments in varying dimensions. Unstable interest rates make investors rethink their investment decisions. Rising interest rates have adverse effects on investments that carry large debt, derivatives, and stock prices, as investors find it difficult to borrow money to finance their investments. Derivatives led to the sinking of some large organizations, for example, Enron. As interest rates rise, the cost of borrowing money rises. Again, the investment's earning decreases as well as its ability to grow. When a company's profitability decreases, its stock becomes less attractive, leading to a decline in the price of stock or outright investment failure.

Generally effective corporate tax has an adverse effect on aggregate investment, FDI (foreign direct investment), and entrepreneurial activities. An increase in corporate tax has a negative effect on growth and positive correlation with informal economy. Lower tax rates can positively stimulate investors and lead to an increase in investment and consumer spending, consequently causing a rise in capital stock.

Fluctuation in the exchange rate has enormous implications on FDI. It reduces the cost of production, profitability, and worker earnings in countries where exchange rates are low compared to countries where there is a high exchange rate. The aim of this part of the book is to reinforce the argument that policymakers or those who run the economy have direct responsibility in the failure and success of investments. Low returns on investments scare investors and might lead to lack of future investments and investment failure. Research revealed that a shift from sound macroeconomic principles by those who run the economy of various nations has contributed to the failure of numerous investments. In the present dispensation and in relation to global investment situation, the position of the author is that until investor confidence and consumer spending is restored, the world will not witness a rise in investment. Indispensably, in the restoration of the investors' confidence and consumer spending, the policymakers play a significant role. Here lies the dilemma.

Accounting and Investment

Accounting refers to the act of collecting, analysing, and disseminating financial information. Accountants analyse and communicate this financial information through balance sheets, the record of financial transactions of a business enterprise for a specific period. The balance sheet is the most important document used by financial officers and institutions for decision making. Finance concerns the sourcing of funds for business and its investment. If the balance sheet is an indispensable document in the financial and investment decision-making process, especially in the area of stocks, mergers, acquisitions, etc., any inconsistency (due, for example, to the greed of the owners or pressure on managers) in the balance sheet will affect the business decision. However, this document, as important as it is in the process of organizational decision making and investments, is not perfect. In this regard, it is worthy to note and to warn investors that taking a company's financial statements at face value can be 'a recipe for disaster'. Part of the imperfection of a balance sheet as a valuable document for financial and investment decision making could be attributed to the complexities surrounding the preparation of the balance sheet and the lack of global standards and procedures.

Although numerous conventions exist for the harmonisation of balance sheets and other financial reports (e.g., income and cash flow statements), they are simply conventions – so as stringent as they might be, they are not judicially redressable especially at a universal level. For a document to be binding on all and sundry universally, it should be judicially enforceable universally with the same legal procedure and requirement, such as, the international court of justice located at Hague. Among these conventions are business entities, historic costs, prudence, going concern, and dual-aspect conventions. While prudence convention holds that "caution should be exercised when making accounting judgements, historic cost convention holds that the value of assets shown on the balance sheet should be based on their acquisition cost (that is, historic cost)" (McLaney and Atrill, 2008, 56). Going by the above definitions, the convention itself creates loophole. Certain figures and issues are based on the judgement and evaluation by the professional, as it is difficult to establish the facts; again, using the historic cost convention, it becomes doubtful to ascertain the actual cost of assets even in the application of a depreciation formula. The question then is to what extent can we trust these professional? Experience has shown that they do the bidding of the paymasters. Investment decisions are therefore not safe in the hands of these professional, as we will establish later.

International financial reporting standards exist to enable investors and the general public to compare the performance of different organizations operating in different countries and organizational setups. The international financial standards were developed by the International Accounting Standards Board (IASB) in the United Kingdom to serve as a single global rule and standard for preparing financial statements. However, as usual with most conventions, various countries have not ratified or adopted some of these accounting conventions, therefore making universal harmonisation or legislation impossible. The IASB was established to police the adoption and harmonisation of these accounting conventions, but the job is still incomplete considering the difficulties that usually exist in the realisation of such global task. Although the situation is the same in many other professions, the difference is that today's investors, as well as financial agents and institutions, participate globally in stocks, bonds, and foreign exchange markets from the comfort of their living room using a laptop. The impending danger then is that if the information in the financial reports are correct, the investors' decision and financial counselling could fail or be successful based on their instinct, experience, and wisdom to the contrary "deceptive or fraudulent accounting practices often conduct to drastic consequences" (Diana and Madalina, 2008).

Although business is associated with risk, there is a clear demarcation between the risk associated with business and a gamble, and outright fraud. Humans are egoistic in nature. An accountant operates in an atmosphere of absolute liberty to prepare financial reports for a company that desires his services. The information and material the accountant is working on are usually collected and submitted by the manager, who has a vested interest in the business. The report is prepared for public assessment of the company. Negative figures highlight the failure of the company and management (although not in every situation), while positive reports will signify the success, hard work, and excellence, and lead to possible promotion for management. From this simple analysis, the tendency is that the possibility of a compromised financial report is very high. The risk and danger is that using the report for assessment of the organization will be misleading and sometimes spell doom for the users and decision makers. Oftentimes, investment failure is traceable to lack of firsthand information regarding the investment before decision making. The outcome is that investors sometimes invest their capital in an organization that looks healthy on paper but bankruptcy in the real world.

The sorry tale of Parmalat, an Italian dairy and food company, and Enron, an American energy, commodities, and services company, are clear examples of 'creative accounting', which will be discussed later in more detail. "Problems of comparability can also occur, as accounting is not a precise science. Judgements and estimates must be made when preparing financial statements, and these may hinder comparisons. Furthermore, no two companies are identical, and the accounting policies adopted may vary between companies for various reasons" (McLaney and Atrill 2008, 161).

Our focus thus far has been towards the explanation of the financial, macroeconomic, and accounting principles and policies in relation to investments. These fundamental principles cannot be overlooked in the discussion and analysis of most financial crises and consequent investment failures, especially the current crises. Obviously the root causes of the failure of most investment is traceable to financial or economic problem, while the causes of financial and economic crises could be mostly attributed to the failure or wrong application of financial, economic, and accounting models, as discussed above.

Although there are many other factors that can lead to the failure of investments, these factors are outside the scope of this book. (Such factors include management issues, environmental situations, command or open-market economies, tariffs, government policies, etc.)

The next chapter deals with the evaluation of the effects of the present financial and economic crises on investments and the financial environment.

CHAPTER 3

Effects of the Crisis

Effects of the Crisis on the Financial Market

I realised the current economic and financial crises had a devastating effect on investments, financial institutions, and its environment. Malcolm, the deputy governor of an Australian central bank, once argued that, "*At its core, the crisis originated in credit markets in developed countries – centred particularly in the United States and subsequently the United Kingdom and Europe – but the fallout has had a significant effect on activities in every country and region*".

The credit crisis is inarguably one of the greatest threats to financial systems in recent time. It has produced unavoidable volatility in the financial market and unprecedented huge losses to investors. From the banking industry to investment companies, bonds markets to derivates, stock prices to commodity markets, all were affected directly or indirectly and suffered one difficulty after another. Rumours generate speculation, and speculation has always had a serious effect on the financial market because it creates fear, tension, and uncertainty.

By the middle of 2007 and through 2008, the effect of the crisis was already visible and spreading like wildfire among the ever-increasing interconnected nations of the world. It was almost certain that the crisis would affect the livelihood of everyone on earth, high and low, rich and poor. Around the globe, stock markets had collapsed, and various financial institutions had fallen, creating untold hardships for the global economy. The US subprime mortgage market crashed, and the reversal of the housing boom in other industrialized economies had a ripple effect on the world's economies. At one point, it became obvious that the world economy has slipped into a deep recession, probably the worst recession after the Great Depression of the 1930s. It was expected that the UK's economy would contract by 4.3 per cent in fiscal year 2009 reported BBC (2009). Also, the world's largest economy, the United States, contracted by 4.1 per cent between 2007 and 2009. Again in the United States, the household spending dropped by 1.2 per cent in the year 2009, the worst recorded since the end of the Second World War (Chandra, 2010).

Taking a closer look at the bond market, it was obvious that at the beginning of the crisis, investors started avoiding risky assets in favour of safer options, like US treasury securities. To attract investors, most financial institutions had to apply an option-adjusted spread (OAS) (where investors demand additional compensation for purchasing a corporate bond, as opposed to ultra-safe treasury securities). After a long period of relative stability between 2003 and mid-2007, the OAS soared to a record high at the beginning of 2008 and dramatically increased as the crisis intensified between the third and final quarters of 2008. The consequent effect of this sharp volatility of the OAS transformed into large losses for the banks and investors and also created large borrowing cost for companies trying to raise capital.

In the United States, as well as in many other countries, the bond market reacted negatively to the prevailing circumstances. In simple terms, the bond yield curve sloped. As the investors hustled to sell risky assets, they scrambled to buy the safety of US treasury bills, bunds, Canadian savings bonds, and the like. This pressure pushed the yield curve for the US treasury securities downwards. During this credit crisis, the yield of a two-year US treasury bond dropped from above 5 per cent to less than 1 per cent, according to the US treasury department. The pressure was more on shorter-term securities at a time the yield of some shorter-term bonds were in negative figures. The only explanation is that 'investor confidence' was at its lowest point. Investors preferred to pay the treasury to keep their money rather than invest in anything that would attract returns. Most investments in certain market and bonds at the time seemed a risk, and most investors were not ready for such a gamble.

The reaction of the stock market to the volatility created by the crisis was nonetheless of equal proportion as the bond market. The rise in the stock prices had been relatively stable, reaching their peak in November 2007. Events took a dramatic turn following the bankruptcy of Lehman Brothers in September 2008. Although the stock prices had been declining since reaching their peak in 2007, the selling intensified as a result of the crisis of Lehman Brothers. The failure of the US House of Representatives to pass the treasury's bailout plan on 29 September did not help matters either.

On the eve of this rejection, the Standard and Poor's (S&P) 500 dropped 8.8 per cent. This was the largest one-day percentage drop by the S&P since 19 October 1987, when the Dow Jones industrial average lost about 22 per cent in a day. (This single event marked the beginning of the stock market decline globally. That day was later referred to as 'Black Monday' and probably still remains the most notorious event in recent financial history.) Also on that faithful day, the total loss of the US stock market was more than one trillion dollars. That was the first time the US stock market would record such a huge loss on a single day.

The decline in the stock market was almost universal. The situation in Europe and Asia was the same as in the United States, as they recorded major declines in prices. On other countries, such as Russia and Hong Kong, their stock markets fell even further. Even the best performer among large stock markets like Mexico declined to 33 per cent as of November 2008.

The consequences for investors was that there was no safe haven because investors seeking refuge from falling markets had nowhere to run to. At this point, it would be necessary to take a closer look at the impact of the market volatility on the investor to understand the behaviour of the investors.

Investors' Confidence

The most important and visible reflection of the financial meltdown was the poor and disastrous performance of the stock and bond market that followed. Obviously more important, although less visible then, was what was happening to the investors' confidence.

The basis of the modern global financial market depends on trust and confidence of the investors. This sensibility is oftentimes derailed by speculation. If this trust and confidence is removed, a dollar bill remains and will be seen as a piece of paper, while a stock certificate will hold no value and be as useful as any other sheet of paper. The credit crisis brought this dangerous dimension to the financial market because 'trust was dramatically affected and finally died down' (Sendanyoye, 2009). Investors began questioning the solvency of banks and other financial markets. If banks and other financial institutions were not able to meet their long-term fixed expenses and maintain long-term expansion and growth, how could they fulfil their obligation to investors? This was the most critical aspect of the crisis because the erosion of confidence consumed the very foundation of the modern financial market. Herein lies the reason the credit crisis posed such a great threat to the financial market and, consequently, the world economy.

Although this fact was slightly treated earlier in this book, it has to be revisited as it is one of the good indicators of the level of confidence. This is because, as confidence cannot be as easily measured as the movements of stocks or bonds, the London Interbank offered rate (LIBOR) came into place to establish the erosion of confidence, at least during the financial crisis (LIBOR is the rate large global banks accept to lend money to each other for a short-term period.) During normal situation, large banks present little credit risk, therefore the relationship between LIBOR and the movement of short-term US treasury security is minimal. LIBOR is rarely discussed or known outside the bond market for this purpose, despite the fact that an enormous loan of about $10 trillion is related to it. It is worthy to note that estimates say that worldwide, a total of $150 trillion of financial products – in both the business and consumer sectors – are indexed to the LIBOR.

However, at the peak of the credit crisis, LIBOR formed an important area of discussion in the mainstream, as well as an important indicator of the global credit freeze. After remaining stable for more than three months, the offered rate fluctuated and increased sharply following the bankruptcy of Lehman Brothers in September 2008. The hike reflected the increasing unwillingness among banks to lend money to each other.

This created serious concern among global policymakers and revealed that the global financial system was heading for a dramatic downturn, apparently because the global economy is based on credit and trust. The turbulence of the LIBOR was short-lived because of the combined actions of the global policymakers that alleviated the fear among the financial market participants. Actually following the sharp increase, LIBOR dropped dramatically in October 2008. Following the central bank's interest rate cut, LIBOR fell below where it was at the onset of the Lehman Brothers bankruptcy.

In summation, I have analysed the effects of the financial crisis on the financial sector and the subsequent reactions of the market. The author also observed that the financial market witnessed an unprecedented turmoil and dramatic decline on the value of many assets. Particular too was the erosion of confidence on the part of the market participants and investors, which sparked serious concern on the part of policymakers and led to their imminent intervention. The next step will be a review of how the crisis affected a few other sectors.

The Effects of the Financial Crises on the Energy Sector

Among the worst hit by the present financial crisis is the energy sector. The energy investment depreciated worldwide as a consequence of the tougher financial environment, thereby weakening the final demand for energy and decreasing cash flow. Especially in fiscal year 2009, the sharp decline in the demand for energy led to the decrease in the international prices of oil, natural gas, and coal. This imbalance created by the decrease in the demand for energy led to a consequential decrease in the supply. This decrease in alternative energy demands is related to a corresponding decrease in the spending on energy-using appliances, vehicles, and equipment by households and businesses alike. Again there was an important knock on effect for efficiency of energy use by end-users. The supply and demand side investment in the energy sector were affected. The energy companies started drilling fewer oil and gas wells while cutting back investments on refineries, pipelines, and power stations. Many of the ongoing investments in this sector are being reviewed; some have been postponed or suffered outright cancellation while others have slowed down production. The reason for the rethinking of these projects is traceable to lack of finance or the downward revision of the projected initial profitability.

While the financial crisis is encouraging end users to restrain in spending across the board as defensive measure, stringent credit conditions and low prices undoubtedly make investment in energy sector savings less attractive. The effect is the delaying of the deployment of a more modern and efficient generation of tools and equipment. Also, the hardware and equipment producers are expected to react through the reduction of investment in research and development, as well as the commercialization of more energy-efficient models, and it seems to be happening. However, this could be salvaged by government intervention through aids. The whole sector is becoming less attractive because of the corresponding decrease in the supply-and-demand effect. "The global upstream oil and gas investment budgets for the year 2009 had already been cut by around 21 per cent compared to 2008 – a reduction of almost $100 billion. Also, between October 2008 and April 2009, more than twenty planned large-scale upstream oil and gas projects valued at a total of more than $170 billion and involving around 2 mb/d of oil production capacity and 1 bcf/d of gas capacity were deferred indefinitely or cancelled" (Birol, 2009)[6].

Effects of the Crises on Financial-Sector Workers

It is obvious that at the centre of the current economic and financial crises are the financial institutions and its affiliates. Among the worst affected by the crises are financial-sector employees. The shakeup in the sector was so immense and imposing that the layoffs announced from 2007 through 2009 amounted to about 325,000 jobs. The figure does not include layoffs from independent mortgage brokers, other independent contractors, or

---

[6] Effects of the financial crises on oil sector: http://www.iea.org/ebc/files/impact.pdf

the rest of innumerable mini financial firms that might not have the resources to combat the crises. Given the fact that mutual trust had been lost among the banking institutions, and interbank lending had also been badly affected, towards the middle of 2008 most British banks started offering their top rates only to those customers that approached them directly. This action restricted the number and type of mortgages available on the market.

So far we have covered the root causes and effects of the present financial crises that have reshaped the global financial market, institutions, and investments. The next chapter will be a review of the economic social and legal implications of failed investments.

CHAPTER 4

Economic Implications of the Failed Investment

Economic Implications of Failed Investments

When an investment fails, probably as a result of poor management, technological advancement and change, poor financing, environmental change and difficulties, etc., there are always severe consequences on the side of investors, the environment, and the employee. These consequences could take the form of job termination, loss of capital and properties on the side of the investors, lack of money to meet immediate needs, as well as social and psychological problems. These problems could be economical, social, and legal or numerous others that do not fall under the scope of this book.

However, it is worthy to note that the crisis, as enumerated earlier, is of great importance in the present and actual conditions. More and more people are losing their jobs, more and more companies are degenerating into bankruptcy, governments are in debt, and the private and public sectors are facing serious problems of liquidity leading to closures. However, when several investments fail simultaneously and probably for the same reason as the subprime mortgage and subsequent bankruptcy like Lehman Brothers, it becomes a crisis.

Although the consequences of the failure of numerous investments are the same as the failure of a single investment, the effect is different. The difference is that the simultaneous failures of many investments create fear among investors. Usually the thinking is that, since the cause of investment failure (investment failure' is hereby defined as A financial investment that has stopped to operate in the way it was initially outlined in the investment contract and record or terms and conditions of the investment agreements) is the same, the tendency is that other investments will follow suit. This thought creates panic among the investors, and panic leads to speculation. The panic and resultant speculation create tension in the market, leading to capital flight, lack of further investments, or outright withdrawal of capital from the market. The result then is financial crisis, and financial crisis triggers economic crisis. It is not wrong to say that financial and economic crises are interrelated.

This part of the book will take a global view of the economic implications of the financial crisis, or put another way, the failure of investments. The author of this book holds the view that one of the economic implications of failed investments, which is clearly visible in the ongoing crisis, is that it reshapes the aggregate supply and demand of goods and services. (Aggregate demand, a.k.a. demand for the gross domestic product [GDP] is the total amount of goods and services demanded in the economy at a given overall price level and at a given time period.) Aggregate demand is usually represented by the aggregate demand-curve, which describes the relationship between the price level and quantity of output that firms are willing to supply to the market. The reshaping or alternation of the aggregate demand leads to fluctuations in the market or financial shock. Market fluctuations spontaneously lead to the reshaping or realignment of the economic variables from their original values. Interest rate, growth rate, unemployment rate, inflation rate, exchange rate, and all the other relevant economic variables will be shaken up as a result of financial shock.

In certain countries, special rules and regulations exist to assist investors with failed investments. An example is Australia, where a special rule called a 'deeming exemption' assists people with failed investments. The rule states that a person can be assisted by the hardship rule depending on each individual's particular circumstances. It implies that if a person has his or her rate of payment assessed under the income test, he or she might be able to have the loan exempted from deeming. The point is that investment failure causes severe hardship to the investor, and some governments are already taking up curative measures to curb the economic hardship and relevant problems that might follow the event of failed investments.

As stated in the previous chapter, one of the economic implications of financial crises is that it leads to the realignment of economic variables. These variables create rigidities that make their adjustment or correction by macroeconomist or policymakers difficult and in some situation impossible. As is the case with the present crisis, most countries are living with large deficits or debt. The financial crisis led to high unemployment rate, poor growth rate, and inflation. In some of these situations, adjustments of the variables become difficult because a country with large debt cannot embark on task reduction to stimulate spending or growth in the same way a country with high inflation cannot embark on monetary contraction to regulate inflation because it will stifle growth or investment and create more unemployment in the long run.

It has been discussed earlier that policymakers adopt macroeconomic measures to correct variables. A country suffering inflation can embark on monetary contraction, while a country suffering unemployment or poor growth can embark on monetary expansion or adjust interest rates to stimulate investment and spending.

In a general economic context, the objectives of the economic policy, which constitute the economic macro-stabilization synergy, are the following: obtaining economic growth; price stability; decrease of unemployment rate; and sustainability of public finance (sustainable budgetary deficit and public debt). Crisis creates rigidity and makes the adoption of these macroeconomic measures difficult and sometimes counterproductive. Although as a corrective measure, some orthodox economists argue that market 'automatic stabilizers' will simultaneously push the economic variables back to their fundamental values once the financial shock is absorbed and the various rigidities have vanished. Part of the flaw of this argument is that the orthodox economist did not take into consideration the strength of the rigidities, externalities, and market imperfections. The point is that some countries have higher inflation rates than others, while others have a higher debt burden. Also, there are those with very high unemployment rates.

Another demerit of the argument is that they did not explain how the rigidities are going to disappear. However, Keynes's theory in contrast to the mainstream economist affirmed that fundamental uncertainty inhibits self-regulating mechanism (Keynes 1936). I am not an advocate of Keynes's theory, but I agree with this argument for obvious reasons.

The point of this argument is that long-term interest rates will never adjust automatically to ensure equilibrium between savings and investments. Also, aggregate demand will not adjust spontaneously to aggregate supply for goods, therefore production and employment decisions adopted by firms and organizations will have to be adopted in relation with their expected demands. This is the reality in the real world of investment. The position of the author is that since markets do not recover on their own, apparently because there is no natural force that guarantees automatic adjustment. The worst economic decision to take after or during a financial crisis, especially the current one that started in 2007, would be to wait blindly for an automatic return to a natural order, as most European governments seem to be doing on the basis of the mainstream's recommendations.

Italy, under Giulio Tremonti, is an example of such countries waiting for a spontaneous return to natural order. Evidently, in the absence of any natural anchor for individual expectation, as usually is the case, it is the conventional views concerning the future that drive liquidity preference and thereby the equilibrium levels of interest rates and asset prices (Lang and Asensio, 2010). This is a reaffirmation of the position of this book.

One of the implications of most crises, including the current financial one, is low wages, which can occur as a result of layoffs, reduction in work hours, or outright termination. The wage decreases or low wages may trigger a negative effect on the marginal efficiency of capital and expected aggregate demand, including aggregate consumption and disposable income, which could lead to cumulative depression. The summary of this argument is that lower wages depress investment (because of low consumption capacity and spending) that decrease the entrepreneur's expectation, thereby leading to lower aggregate demand and, consequently, supply.

It can be convincingly argued that the amount of a stimulus package put up by most countries to combat the effect of the crisis is insufficient. In view of the crisis and in the consideration of the response by EU authorities, it is evidently clear that the EU efforts have borne little progress so far as the economic recession, and the financial crises have become reinforcing events, causing EU government to offer large policy responses. The poor growth and stagnant economic situation in most European countries are evidences of this insufficiency. Despite the series of interventions by most central banks directed towards the removal of toxic assets from the market and thereby reassuring the market and investors, the financial system continues to be weakened by the depreciation of the stock of many bad debts that negatively affect financial institutions' balance sheets.

Insofar as bad debts are recycled and not recovered or recognized as losses, the situation will remain the same for another long period, especially when nobody can say for sure that all the junk bonds have been discovered. This is obviously the problem of securitization, which has been discussed earlier (see chapter 2). The recirculation of debts (among which, many had been severally recirculated) has made it impossible for financial institution to know how many junk bonds they have on their balance sheets. Although this will continue to pose a destabilizing effect in the financial market, the most critical aspect of the problem is that it will continue to reduce the confidence of investors as well as the market. The capacity of governments and central banks to support or control the financial system will continue to be in doubt, especially in relation to pulling the junk bonds out of the system.

Another important aspect of the problem created by the crisis is that the memory of collapse will continuously haunt the policymakers and investors. The fear is that this will curb all risk-taking investment decisions. Particularly the entrepreneurs' decision making may be affected. The problem is that these decisions are connected to long-term financing of productive sectors and operations and precisely the long-run investment decisions in the real-world economy. This is the reality of the present financial condition because despite the intervention of the government and the central banks over the last few years, banks and other financial institutions continue to refuse the financing of numerous private projects. Worse still is that it is becoming increasingly more difficult for entrepreneurs to finance new projects, even when the risk involved is reasonable.

Unfortunately, there seems to be no way out of this problem, at least not in the near future, especially when household attitude towards investments and savings seem to favour low-risk investments. This is because the relative price of money compared with risky assets – especially the long-term interest rate – tends to remain at high levels, at least for private borrowers and investors. The effect is that household investments in housing and durable goods, including the productive investments of firms become too expensive, thereby weakening aggregate demand, production level, and potential output. It will not be wrong to insist that aggregate demand is going to remain low for some time, simply because aggregate demand is the result of entrepreneurs' expectations, among other things. From all available evidences, there is nothing that suggests entrepreneurs' expectations will be optimistic in the near future. Where the expectation about the future is pessimistic, the tendency is that investments are contained or stopped. Again, a depreciation of expected return on productive investment can be expected, not only because of a continuous decrease in demand for household goods but because more and more people continue to suffer unemployment, and many others reach a stage where unemployment benefits are terminated.

Another point that deserves attention is that the reduction in the demand for investment and the consumption of household goods is enlarged by the negative effect of the economic depression on wages and income. The point is that since the decreasing of wages and continued high unemployment rate leads to cumulative depressive forces, the stability of the economy can be achieved only through the capacity of the labour market and institutions to stop continued wage decline and address unemployment. Part of the good news is that in most capitalist economies, the nominal wage seems to be relatively stable as people and institutions tends to resist wage reduction despite high unemployment rate and financial difficulties. Indeed, the world economy is already living under a high unemployment regime.

The rate of unemployment in the United States in 2011 was 9.2 per cent. As of June 2014, it is still a staggering 6.3 per cent. In a country like Italy, unemployment of youths stood at about 23 per cent in the first quarter of 2011. In the southern part of Italy, the situation was worst. The tendency is that the situation will remain the same for quite some time, even if the world economy starts experiencing recovery – that is, the appreciation of the growth rate like we presently have in Germany.

The major concern of the author is that, even with modest growth, the memory of the crisis and fear of the unknown may continue to haunt investors and firms for some time. Therefore, they might adopt a 'wait and see' attitude or increase prices instead of hiring new employees. Given the situation of high unemployment and low growth, most countries suffering high unemployment due to political pressure may embark on mass economic stimulus or policy reform as no real recovery can take place under such conditions. The thinking and conviction of the author is that no lasting recovery (return of investment) can take place, except the confidence of investors is restored, especially with regards to profitability of investment and aggregate demand. It will take the combined effort and action of the authorities and economic institutions to achieve an optimistic view on the side of the investor.

Prior to the financial crisis in 2008, a lot of wealth had been created and circulated. A major part of this excess wealth had been exchanged for the private debts, while part of them were absolved by the rush to liquidity and secure holdings. This excess liquidity was money that fed the housing bubble. (This issue has been discussed previously but is represented here because it was one of the root causes of the crisis and because it will be instrumental to the regulation of inflation and monetary policy and serve as resolution of the crisis.)

Following the recovery of the financial sector in 2009, part of the money might have penetrated the stock market, while another substantial part had gone into the world economy, especially through securitization. In a normal situation, this wouldn't pose a problem, but in a crisis situation, where the money supply – which transforms into purchasing power – injected into the system over some time do not find corresponding value of goods and services at the previous rate. The pressure of the excess liquidity in the financial market and world economy including expansionary policies of most government could trigger inflation.

Given the second face of the crisis, it will be difficult for the producers to provide the amount of goods, necessary to absorb the liquidity including the ones circulated by the banks. As a follow-up to this crisis, the fiscal policy of most countries could take different dimensions. The reason is that most countries might pay attention to inflation while others may choose to worry more about low growth rate based on the political and social pressure in each given state. This is the situation of EU under the current leadership of Jean-Claude Juncker (despite UK and Hungary opposition Juncker was nominated the European Commission president by the rest 26 members in June 2014 for a five year tenure). Although given the reduced income of most states as a result of reduced tax, the pressure could be on most states to embark on the balancing of the budget.

This pressure could be from the rating agencies, considering how they treated countries like Greece and Portugal in 2010, or institutions like the European Union (EU) that pay serious attention to budget deficit. This is already happening. In September 2011, Standard and Poor's declared the Italian state had drifted from stable to negative, the last downgrade of Italy by Standard and Poor's was in June 2014. In July 2014, Moody's followed suit by declaring that the Italian banks were in distress. One of the banks affected is the biggest Italian bank, also the second-largest bank in Europe, the UniCredit Bank[7].

The rating agency did not spare the United States, and Moody's sounded a note of warning that if immediate measures are not taken, the country could default. In August 2011, Standard and Poor's downgraded US credit rating for the first time. Other rating agencies followed suit; some in 2011 while others downgraded US rating in subsequent year. Twice since the inception of the crisis, US president Barak Obama has held meetings with the opposing party (Republicans) to increase their deficit level to prevent the country from defaulting. The negotiation is still

---

[7] Moody's rating agency downgraded Italian Bank Unicredit (https://www.moodys.com/research/Moodys-downgrades-Italian-banks--PR_250584)

ongoing, but the puzzle is that nobody can predict how it is going to end, and the resolution does not bring an end to the impending danger facing the United States.

The balancing of the budget already embarked on by various countries could worsen the scenario as it is going to put severe pressure on the general public. The result will probably be an L-shaped depression (when an economy has a severe recession and does not return to trend-line growth for many years, if ever). Usually recession comes with increasing pressure on expenses and reduced income. Because expenditures remain the same, businesses and investments are usually under intense pressure, and many entrepreneurs may go out of business as income is reduced because customers have tightened or closed their pockets.

As lenders struggle to recover, bad debts' interest rates increase, and those seeking loans to finance their business may find it difficult to find new sources. New investments are hindered by lack of funds and fear of the unknown.

My position is that, the future of investments is still bleak. The next chapter will explore the social implications of the crisis.

CHAPTER 5

Social Implications of the Failed Investment

The Social Implication of the Crisis

The financial crisis inevitably led to the closing of many businesses and financial losses on the side of investors, business owners, and institutions. The loss of capital and the closing of businesses led to layoffs and job terminations, as well as lack of funds for new investments. Jobs are still the missing link in the outlook for recovery. The result is the lack of creation of new jobs, the shrinking of the GDP, and a reduction in aggregate supply and demand. Worse still is that the fear of the crisis and failure of investments continue to haunt the investors, leading to the pulling out of money from the banks.

Because banks reinvest or give out as loans the money collected from customers, it sometimes becomes difficult for banks to refund this money on demand, especially when there is a rush for withdrawal. The inability of the banks to refund money to depositors has a negative effect as it continues to lead to the loss of confidence and fear on the part of the investor and depositors.

Part of the weakness of the present global economy is that because of the interconnectedness of the financial system, what is happening in one country has an immediate impact on the rest of the world. Although these issues have been extensively discussed previously in this book, they are represented here as a basis to addressing social issues. There is a direct correlation between financial crises (investment failure) and unemployment, as financial crises depress the economy through the closure of businesses, thereby leading to job losses.

Taking Britain as an example because Britain is a crucial hub in the global financial system, the British economy contracted by 4.5 per cent in the 2010 fiscal year. Among the fallout of the crisis was the nationalization of a bank like the Royal Bank of Scotland. Considering that the British economy is deeply reliant on finances, at least in recent years, such measures, like recapitalization, had a devastating effect on the image of the financial institutions and the economy.

Although London, inarguably one of the financial leaders of the world, did not cause the crisis, it has received more than its fair share of the pain. The major problem facing Britain as well as the global economy is how to emerge from one of the toughest challenges of the decade. At the beginning of 2010, it had cost Britain about £860 billion of taxpayers' money to support the banks, and about 60,000 financial services jobs had been lost. This is partly because the economy before the crisis had been fuelled by debt (most of which were bad), and as a result, most banks went into hardship and the financial market immediately seized up.

Prevention of a reoccurrence of the crisis means tightening or adjusting the way banks and financial institutions conduct business. Financial institutions are now undergoing more scrutiny in their duties, especially in the way they extend risk to others. The consequence is that while holding more assets and capital will make banks less risky, it will lead to less money in circulation. Incidentally the British government had increased tax by 50 per cent on the bonuses paid to most bankers, and a higher income tax may follow. This might lead to an exodus of bankers and financial workers from Britain. How and when this is going to happen is yet unknown, but the fact is, tax increment eventually lead to less disposable income and a reduction in purchasing power.

Unemployment creates social problem as it leads to lack of funds for day-to-day running and upkeep of the family. Unemployment often leads to an increase in the crime rate. According to Eurostat crime statistics, while violent crime like homicide, robbery, property crime and drug trafficking were in the decrease between 2007 and 2012 domestic burglary increased by 14 per cent within the same period[8].

Part of the problem with the unemployment rates published by most countries and institution is that they fail to take into account the fact that in most situations, especially in Europe, most of the unemployed have lost faith in the system and therefore had stopped searching for jobs. The result is that the records of those people that have stopped seeking employment have been deleted from the labour register, and it becomes difficult to get the true figure of the unemployment rate. However, unemployment rates had reached all-time high in most countries.

As of November 2009, New York City lost about 170,000 workers to unemployment. In this same period, the unemployment figure for United States stood at 5.9 million. This is about 4.4 per cent of the total population of the city, and 38.3 per cent of the unemployed in the United States. In September 2010, the figure had increased to more than double, reaching a total of 413.000 unemployed about 10.3 per cent of the population in New York. About 40,000 of the people that lost their jobs are living on the street (Hewitt, 2010). These figures refer to the city centre alone because in the periphery of the city, the crisis has more serious social effect. Consider the Brooklyn neighbourhoods predominantly dominated by African Americans, where the unemployment rate stands at about 20 per cent, this fact becomes clearly evident. The figure released by the Italian social security department (INPS) on 14 July 2011 stated that about eight million Italians are living below poverty level. About three million of these same people live in a state of abject poverty, meaning these people cannot afford three square meals a day, not to mention reaching the end of the month financially.

These figures clearly tell the tale of how bad the failure of investments has socially affected the population of some of the world's foremost economies. New York City, which is considered the world hub of financial

---

[8] Erostate Crime Statics recorded a rise in crime rate (http://epp.eurostat.ec.europa.eu/statistics_explained/index.php/Crime_statistics#Total_recorded_crime)

and commercial activities, had been employing about 351,000 people in the financial and insurance sectors alone, but this figure has drastically reduced to 313,000 after the bankruptcy and financial collapse of the Lehman Brothers. This figure represents 11 per cent of the financial workers pushed to the unemployment market.

To alleviate the social difficulty of these laid off Wall Street workers, reintegration or transitioning them into new fields like education and social services New York had drawn eleven million dollars from national emergency funds.

As is the case with most cities, each city has a symbol or features that make the city significant. What makes Venice significant is tourism as well Paris is noted for luxury shops. The pressure of the crisis created serious effects on these features for which those cities are noted, significantly because the crisis has left less funds in the pocket of people, therefore social life receives less attention.

While tourism has suffered a serious decrease in Venice, nightlife has reduced by 0.3 per cent between 2009 and 2010. About 41 per cent of people revealed they eat in cheaper establishments, or enjoy snacks or take-away meals while 19 per cent have removed alcohol from their meal. The bottom line is that all these lead to less income and eventual closure of most restaurants and social operators, at least the luxurious ones (Elan, 2009). The closures will lead to more layoffs and unemployment. Although the situation will lead to the springing up of cheaper establishments and fast food restaurants, the emergence of cheaper establishment is a confirmation of the social effect of the crisis.

Another striking revelation is that about 38 per cent of New Yorkers say that along with offering better services, they are now more appreciated when they go to restaurants (Fitzpatrick, 2010). This is a sign that things are harder than they used to be and that customers are now more valuable as they become harder to come by. The situation is not different as attendance to pricey Broadway shows has dropped 9.3 per cent while traffic to the museums has greatly appreciated. The museums offer another cheap opportunity of enjoyment in the city, which explains how deep the crisis had eaten into the purses of New Yorkers.

Between the summer of 2008 and February 2009, employment in the arts and entertainment industry dropped from seventy-one thousand to sixty-four thousand. The arts and entertainment sector defines the glamour that New York is made of. The effect of the financial crisis did not spare the rental market either. The singles, which New York is noted for, can now dream of settlements in places like Manhattan during this downturn. These low-income earners in the recent past could have shifted base to Brooklyn or Queens, where they could find cheap accommodations, but they can now aspire with a little sacrifice for the comfort of Manhattan because of a reduction in rental costs due to the crisis. Also the rents in a place like Greenwich Village, the notable home of hedge funds, dropped to about 15.9 per cent in 2009, and locations like Chinatown and Hell's Kitchen became as competitive as Bushwick (Brooklyn) and Astoria (Queens) as they emerged as locations for hipsters. Also, haggling, which had become history, returned.

The financial crisis has drastically reduced the purchasing power of people everywhere on the planet and has affected their social outlook and standing. In most large cities in Europe, there are recent or ongoing protests against the crisis and its eventual consequences.

On 15 May 2011, towards the end of the campaign for the local and administrative election in Spain, about 25,000 young people defied the government ban. They gathered overnight in Madrid (Spain's capital) and occupied the main square. In what is now popularly known as the 'los indignados' ('the indignant'), these young protesters were angry with the government's austerity measures and the high unemployment rate. It was a symptom and expressed a general feeling of concern and anger. The unemployment rate in Spain had soared to an all-time high of 21.3 per cent, affecting about 4.6 million people, the highest in Europe. Among people between the ages of sixteen and twenty-nine, the unemployment rate stands at about 45 per cent. The protest started spontaneously as a sit-in in Puerta del Sol, the main square of Madrid, but instantly spread to other cities like Barcelona, Seville, and Valencia.

What started as a sit-in turned into a protest and later transformed into an occupation. The occupation went on for about six days before the protesters were disbanded due to the Spanish law that banned any protest the day before an election to allow for a day of reflection. The fact that the crowd was camping out in the square overnight shows the extent of the frustration and pain the crisis has caused. What is unique about this protest is that it had no affiliation with any political party or labour unions. This young people organized themselves through Facebook, other social media, and the Internet, a repeat situation of the North African revolt 'Arab Spring'. Arab Spring is a revolutionary wave of demonstrations, protest (sometimes violent) and civil war in the Arab world which began in December 2012 spreading through North African countries and Arab nations.

This crisis has probably led to the emergence of a new type of movement. This is because protests of such magnitude are initially known to be organized by trade unions or political parties. However, what is clear is that something new is happening. Protesters are afraid government intervention will leave them without social amenities like public health and education. They fear an impending danger of lack of employment prospects even for graduates in the near future. All hope seems lost. It would not be wrong to conclude this part by saying that even the loss of the administrative and local election by the ruling socialist party in Spain is a result of fallout from the financial crisis.

In most cities in Europe, the people have to make do with temporary, partial, or short work contracts because of the crisis. Although these types of employment contract offer little or no benefits, the major problem is that they do not give the owners or custodians confidence or guarantees. One cannot plan his or her future on a temporary contract. Most young people no longer think of marriage because the future is not guaranteed. In an ageing society like in Europe, lack of marriage or bearing of children will definitely lead to another social crisis. In a country like Italy, where the pension scheme is pay-as-you-go, it might be difficult to pay retirees' pensions in a few years because the numerical strength of the workers will not be enough to sustain the ever-growing number of pensioners. Such countries may have to resort to immigrants as most countries are already doing, irrespective of the crisis. It remains to be seen whether the immigrants will be enough to sustain all the countries that are in need of an immigrant workforce as a result of the ageing class, as some emerging nations offer better prospects for these immigrants and therefore open another opportunity for immigration. More still, most countries are democratising, as the trend in North Africa has shown. It remains to be seen whether these revolutions have positive or negative effects in the long run.

The financial crisis is leading to an economic realignment as most of the emerging countries are growing at a higher rate than in the West, and the citizens of these migrating countries may not have real need to leave their country after some time. Another observation is that this crisis has created a high level of social imbalance among the citizens almost everywhere in the world. The rich are getting richer and the poor continue to remain poor.

The social implication of the financial crisis in Greece is worse than one can imagine. Since the formal acceptance of the failure of the Greek economy by the government led by Prime Minister George Papandreou, the country has fallen into a protracted crisis. Remarkably, the most severe consequences are being borne not by bondholders but by ordinary Greeks. The economy shrank 5.5 per cent in the first quarter. Unemployment has hit 15.9 per cent, compared with 11.7 per cent just one year ago. Some 30 per cent of Greeks younger than thirty have lost their job. Although protest in Greece has become a recurrent feature at least in recent time, the problematic aspect is that it has transformed into a revolt.

The protest started on 5 May by the direct 'Democracy now' to protest the government plan to cut spending and increase taxes in exchange for the €110 billion bailout aimed at resolving the 2010 and 2011 debt crisis. Tragically, three people lost their lives in the arson that occurred during the protest, seen as the largest in Greece since 1973. The three victims were among the twenty employees of the Marfin Bank branch of Stadiou Avenue in central Athens, where a petroleum bomb was thrown. The rest of the employees managed to escape as the flames grew severe, but the unfortunate three found their way blocked as they tried to escape through the roof, and they suffocated. Attempts to save them yielded no results, as it was difficult to get to the scene because of the protesting crowd. Many other places were set on fire but had no victims. Numerous police officers were wounded during the protest, but the human victim took precedence as the police and protesters accused each other as to what really led to the death of the three people.

The general strike that accompanied the protest was the third in recent months in Greece. The strike paralysed Greece, as flights in and out stopped at midnight, and the trains, buses, and ferries were not running, creating hardship for travellers. The schools and hospitals, and most offices offering essential services were also closed down. The government had to intervene to appeal to staff in the police, military, hospitals, and schools not to resign. The fear in the government circle was that the retirement of these demoralised staffs demanding increased benefit would not only lead to an upsurge in the demand for benefits by others and further crises, but would aggravate the already-weak economy.

The revolt in Greece continued with protests, strike actions, and demonstrations until the past few weeks.

The situation grew worse by the day as more people lost their jobs and more businesses closed. As the income of most people cannot sustain them until the end of the month, the crime rate is in an upsurgence. Others will have to resort to grandparents and other family members or have to borrow. Many still live on credit, which means skipping bills here and there. Most cannot afford to pay their domestic bills, meaning that they have to live days or weeks without lights or gas.

The social situation in Greece and many other parts of the world is that bad. The protest in Greece is now a nearly daily event. On 29 June 2011, there was another round of protests in various cities, including the capital (Athens) as the government considers another round of austerity measures.

Angry citizens protested by hurling flaming debris and rocks on the capital city's street. The police responded by throwing tear gas and shooting rubber bullets at the protesters as the demonstration degenerated into a riot. Many houses were destroyed and cars burnt. Whatever the outcome, the only thing that is clear is that the people are determined to defeat the government – meaning Greece will not know peace, at least in the near future. It is the strong conviction of the author that the student demonstrations in Britain, the riots in Greece, and the union protests in France, Italy, and Belgium were all born of the same frustration and they are all indicators to the extent of the hardship and hopelessness the financial crisis has caused.

The next step, the second-to-last stage of this book, will deal with the legal implications of the crisis.

CHAPTER 6

Legal Implications of Failed Investments

Legal Implication of Failed Investment in Relation to the Financial Crisis

Although the financial crisis started in the United States, it had since extended to every part of the globe because there is no standalone financial crisis. This is because the money and capital markets operate under such a complex situation and an internationally interwoven system with very high dependencies. It is now an established fact that the financial crisis and the consumer credit crunch are two sides of the same coin. It has been extensively treated earlier in this book, but to help draw a line on the legal implication of failed investments, it will be enough to reaffirm that the cause of the crisis is not only a result of the greed of the financial institutions but a follow up of the craze for high returns on investments by institutional and private investors.

Partly the conception that a return of a well-above-average interest rate ratio is not an anomaly contributed to the crisis. This consensus of opinion helped both parties jump the gun. Evidently, towards the end of the 1980s, the central banks of the G10 (Group of Ten refers to a group of eight countries and two central banks who entered into agreement to participate in the General Agreement to Borrow in 1964) attempted to regulate the banking industry and capital market. However, the harder the central banks tried to regulate these institutions, the more they tried to avoid the consequences. The Basel I agreement (the round of deliberations by central bankers from around the world. In 1988, the Basel Committee on Banking Supervision (BCBS) in Basel, Switzerland, published a set of minimum capital requirements for banks) agreed among other regulations to compelling the banks to hold 8 per cent equity capital in comparison to their assets. The subsequent Basel II agreement agreed on the following:

- ➤ Loans have to be connected to the creditworthiness of the customer according to a rigid scoring modus, meaning, in effect, attractive conditions for customers of high standing and harsh conditions for the others.
- ➤ a significant tightening of governmental control of the banking sectors dealings
- ➤ strongly increased transparency regulations for banking strategies and dealings

For obvious reasons, however, incongruent with the norms of the financial business, the regulations stipulated above had never been applied in most countries. It became clearly evident that the United States, the world's greatest power, was dismissing most of the treaty with impunity. Neither the United States nor any world leading financial institution has ever refuted that the main causes of the bubble were loose monetary policy, particularly by the US Federal Reserve, and global imbalances. The combination of cheap credit together with the easy availability of funds contributed to create the bubble.

The criteria did not fit the notorious system of most countries. Rather, in application of the economic principles discussed earlier in this book (stimulating spending), the order of most government has been deregulation. Also important is the manoeuvre that had been going on in the European banking sector. The activities had been directed towards evading the risk, minimizing the Basel I Accord and, consequently, profit-minimizing regulation. This is because the application of Basel Accord leads to a reduction in profit. What we have today under the harsh realities of the financial crisis and the recession is the united efforts of the world governments to reform and regulate financial markets. These efforts were aimed at restoring confidence among banks and between banks and customers. It seems pointless, like administering medicine after death. Summarily, the disbelief in regulations in the United States and the evasion strategy in Europe culminated into the financial crisis and investment failure the world is going through. Again, the so-called tax havens (countries like the Cayman Islands, Virgin Island, Dublin docks in Ireland, etc., with extremely low corporate tax) did not help matters as they provided a sure way to evade the rules and taxes.

For many decades, the asset-backed securities were bundled, sliced, and traded in the financial markets as secured bonds. It was possible because for three decades, the real estate market had only moved upwards. House owners took loans with excellent returns because there was no real estate crisis for many years. Suddenly the bubble burst, and the loans could not be paid; houses collapsed, and asset-backed securities dramatically lost their real value. Among the banking institutions, the money-lending activities stalled as a result of lack of mutual trust. Eventually banks and insurance companies folded, leading to massive government interventions in the financial market. The failure of these investments led to legal demands like the creation of an internationally valid financial supervisory system to close all gaps.

Also among the legal demand were regulations for hedge funds, which currently undergo almost no control mechanisms. This demand was not unfounded considering that hedge funds controlled trillion of dollars and contributed immensely to the worsening of the crisis. Initially the fund was meant to hedge against the interest rate and currency risk, but due to the greed of the investors, it transformed into a financial powerhouse, offering credit in stocks, shares, and currency market.

In no time, the aggressive hedge funds were termed 'vulture funds', and 'short selling' was invented. Inevitably, short selling has brought entire countries almost to the point of collapse, evidently because hedge funds act speculatively and shareholder value-oriented only, abandoning the traditional function of securing real business activities. The currency speculation of the Soros hedge fund against the British pound, which led to the devaluation of pounds, explains the extent of damage such a fund can do. However, the concern of this book in this section is the legal implication of the crisis; therefore, it is important to reiterate that as a follow-up to the failure of investment, short selling was stopped as a first measure in the most important markets (namely the United

States and Europe). Consequently, the supervision over hedge funds was tightened by various governments including EU. The G20 also reached an understanding in this regard. This, I believe, was the beginning of the legal turning point of the necessary activities.

Another legal hiccup in the wake of the financial crisis was the 'investment advisory' business, which led to the implementation of the European regulation in the field of consumer protection. This act led to the gradual enforcement of consumer rights through the filling of standardized profile risk of the investor during the protocol advisory talk. It evaluates whether the investment strategy fits the investment aim. The implication is that consumers have to be fully informed of all the risks inherent with the offered financial product, followed by a written affirmation that he or she was dully informed and understands all the information therein. Also, the banks were compelled not only to offer their own products but to give correct information about competing products and their cost structures to enable the consumer reach a balanced decision. The idea behind this legal requirement was to protect investors, as experience has shown that banks often act as distribution channels of high-risk bonds for issuers during the crisis, as explained below.

The Citibank German branch sold 130,000 Lehman Brothers certificates in 2008 alone. They were sold at the nominal value of 10,000 Euro each as secure certificates. It was later to be revealed that Citibank received tangible kickback premiums from Lehman Brothers for this dirty deal. Also, each Citibank advisor received a bonus for selling a certificate. Although the banks claimed the customers were duly informed, it is just natural that nobody will invest his or her hard-earned money in such a venture, except out of ignorance. As a follow-up to this illicit activity, Citibank was sued by four thousand investors in Belgium, and in Spain they accepted a deal to buy back the issued certificates of twenty-seven hundred investors at 55 per cent of the initial offering.

However, I believe the way out of such a messy situation in the future will be the implementation of a reversal of the burden of proof in relevant laws. This will be applied in the future by compelling the financial institution to prove they properly informed their customers. This is a legal demand that is yet to be approved in most countries.

The general downturn in the financial circle has led to other legal issues. As a result of severe regulations, credit card lines are suffering dramatic cuts, and applicants are turned away in large numbers. Credit card limits have been drastically reduced, and cash balances in many situations are avoided because of high fees and interest rates for using this service. Households with a questionable credit history are also blacklisted for further credit until a more responsible approach if not severe is adopted towards lending. All these measures unintentionally harm consumer confidence and spending as well as the general economy.

Earlier in this book, Parmalat was discussed. (Parmalat SpA is an Italian dairy and food company located in Parma, Italy). Parmalat, like Enron, is an example of a company manipulating the balance sheet and flagrantly flouting accounting principles with impunity. The Parmalat case demonstrates that internal control can be as important outside the US as inside. It also explains the helpless situation investors can find themselves in the endless legal battle to recover their hard-earned money and the extent the greed of the company owners can go in ruining the life of investors.

Let's see how this happened. Two decades after its founding, Parmalat had transformed into a multinational corporation dealing in dairy beverages, baked goods, and other products and was listed in the Milan Stock Exchange in the 1990. By 2002, the company was valued at 3.7 billion euro. Parmalat had 36,000 workers in thirty countries, 140 production centres. Five thousand Italian dairy farms depended on Parmalat for the majority of their business. Parmalat had interest in many other organizations, like Parma football club, Parma Tours, and Odeon TV, to name a few.

Unfortunately, in 2003 Parmalat collapsed and was declared bankrupt, with a 14.3 billion euro hole in their account, the biggest financial shake-up in European history at the time. Parmalat financed several international acquisitions, especially in the Western hemisphere, with debt. Towards 2001, most of the acquisitions were running at a loss, so the company shifted the financing of its operations to the use of derivatives, obviously to cover its debt.

In February 2003, the CFO unexpectedly announced the issue of five hundred million Euro bonds, which led to his resignation, and Alberto Ferraris took over. Ferraris did not have access to some of the corporate books as they were handled by the chief accountant, Luciano Del Soldato. This strange situation led Ferraris to investigate the account, and he later discovered the company's debt was far more than the declared amount. Parmalat's shares depreciated when the plan to raise three hundred million Euro through mutual fund Epicurum was dropped due to public concern. Ferraris resigned a week after the public outcry, and Soldato took over. Soldato resigned a month later after his failure to raise funds from Epicurum to pay the debts and matured bonds coupon totalling 150 million Euro.

This contributed to Parmalat's bankruptcy, and the government took over under Enrico Bondi as CEO after the resignation of Calisto Tanzi the founder and former CEO. Several of the company's subsidiaries went into solvency. Bank of America released a document later that 3.95 billion euros in Parmalat's account were a forgery. The subsequent fraud investigation led to the arrest of Tanzi. Hundreds of thousands of investors lost their money, and many initiated an unending legal battle. Tanzi admitted during questioning that there was an eight billion euro hole in the accounts but said it was not intentional.

However, this figure did not appear on the balance sheets. The auditors later confirmed that the deficit was 14.3 billion euros. Due to the manipulation of accounting practices, Parmalat was rich only on paper. The fact concerning Parmalat, Enron, and Worldcom (other cases of established organized organizational fraud) was that corporate managers engaged in earnings, manipulations and accounting irregularities to inflate the stock price and gain from their equity and options holdings. At Parmalat, family member shareholders had expropriated corporate resources via self-dealing.

The court of Milan sentenced Tanzi to ten years imprisonment for fraud relating to the collapse of Parmalat. Ten years was commuted to eight years, six months. Several executives, including bankers, were discharged and acquitted, while others settled out of court. Lawsuits instituted by

Parmalat finance against Bank of America and auditors were dismissed. As of this date, no investor has recovered his or her money. In Italy, the legal process is enormously long. Most of the investors who initiated legal proceedings may have to wait another long period, although many of them are living in abject poverty.

The rescue of the Northern Rock Bank of London also raised some legal issues. On 14 September 2007, the bank received liquidity support from the bank of England. The bank had gone into liquidity crisis (an acute shortage, or 'drying up', of liquidity. Liquidity is a catch-all term that may refer to several different yet closely related concepts) at the inception of the financial crisis because of its exposure to the US's subprime mortgage market having abandoned its initial finance-raising focus of deposit taking.

The bailout of the bank by the Bank of England had caused panic among depositors, who decided to withdraw their money. The request for withdrawal compounded Northern Rock's liquidity problem. Critics said the Bank of England could not have intervened publicly, although these critics did not suggest a method of intervention that could be hidden from the public and the consequences of such a secret deal. The conflicting legal issues is that of covert market operations, as proposed by the critics and the European market abuse directive, which stipulates in article 6 (i) that "issuers of financial instrument should inform the public as soon as possible of the inside information which directly concerns them". Practical application of this law prevents the central bank from engaging in covert market operations.

However, the European Union (EU) argued that the directive contained two provisions, out of which is a subsection of article 6, which the Bank of England could have relied on for the Northern Rock scenario. This article says an issuer may delay the public disclosure of inside information such as not to prejudice his legitimate interest, provided the issue is able to ensure the confidentiality of that information. But the Bank of England insisted it was caught by article 6 despite the existence of the caveat. Although the argument concerning the bailout of Northern Rock was centred around the market abuse directive, there exists article 87 of the EU rules on state aids, which expressly prohibits any state from granting aids of any form whatsoever (State Aid 1997). It could be argued under common law that the bailout of an entity that ran into liquidity crisis as a result of market problem could not be seen as a state aid. The relevant point is that the failure of Northern Rock and the bailout by the central bank had serious legal implications.

The application of Montreal accord in Canada led to the alleviation of liquidity problem by simple negotiation. It happened that the group of banks, lenders, and funds led by Caisse de Dépôt et Placement du Québec (which manages public pension plans in the Canadian province of Quebec. It was founded in 1965 by an act of the National Assembly) negotiated a proposal known as the Montreal Protocol standstill and agreed to convert trusts' short-term debt into longer-term notes with higher interest rates. The negotiation brokered an accord whereby all the maturity dates of both assets and liabilities were brought into line with one another. However, the adoption of the Montreal Protocol could not have been possible in the Northern Rock crisis because every deal in Europe must be in compliance with the EU competition rules. So an arrangement, whereby organizations agreed to restrict trade in commercial paper, is not tenable under European law as article 81 prohibits any agreement that has as an objective the restriction of competition within the EU. If a competition is a game of 'winner takes all', I believe certain commercial or financial accord like bailouts will simply be a violation of the norm.

CHAPTER 7

Democratic Impediment and Political Implications of the Failed Investment

---

Adam Smith said in his book *The Wealth of Nations*, "It is not from the benevolence of the butcher, the brewer, or the baker that we expect our dinner but from their regard to their own interest". This captivating message captures the egoistic nature of man, who is naturally self–centred; therefore, the agony of leaving our destiny in the hands of other people is sometimes frustrating. This is in consideration of the fact that man is constantly faced with the problem of survival, and his continued existence depends on the extent he is able to solve the numerous problems continuously staring him in the face. Logically, if mankind still exists, one might say man has solved his problem, but that might be true only to an extent. This is because the continuous existence of wants, poverty, and hardship attest to the fact that if man has solved his problems, it is only partial. Man has not been able to achieve paradise on earth and probably never will.

Economics evolved in the continuous search by man to solve his numerous problems. The discussion of whether economics has harmoniously proffered a solution to the problems of mankind is a topic for another day, but if economic activity exists, somebody has to organize, control, or exploit it. Neither man nor economic activity can exist in isolation. Without mincing words, Aristotle said, "An important constituent of happiness is friendship, the bond between the individual and the social aggregation, between man and the State". Man is essentially, or by nature, a social animal; that is to say he cannot attain complete happiness except in social and political dependence on his fellow man. This is the starting point of political science and political philosophy. Suffice it to say that the State is not absolute. This implies that even man is not absolute.

Plato taught that there is no ideal state, that our knowledge of political organization is to be acquired by studying and comparing different constitutions of states, that the best form of government is that which best suits the character of the people. These are notably some of the most characteristic of Aristotle's political doctrines as recorded in the Catholic Encyclopaedia of 1911. The past two thousand years have proved this assertion to be true and went miles ahead to confirm that man is a political animal. It also emphasised the fact that man has to depend on his fellow man for the advancement of mankind.

Humanity cannot make headway without politicians or political activities simply because the majority of policymakers or those who appoint them are politicians. Politicians belong to political parties, and political parties play politics. Politics then is the exercise and theory of influencing other people or organizations on a civic level. More narrowly put, politics is related to the activities of influencing the actions and policies of a government or alternatively getting and controlling power. Relatively controlling power refers to protecting, preserving, and defending power and resource in which micro and macro economic variables are used. These variables are controlled by the government, or more precisely by policymakers. To understand the interrelatedness of politics and investment, let's take a closer look again at some of these factors.

Interest rate plays a significant role in the determination of investment. It could be higher or lower depending on the prospects of a government or the policymakers. The high or low interest rate has a direct effect on investment. This is partly because investment is a process through which capital is increased for use in a later period as circumstances may require. How many a times have we heard that interest rates stimulated borrowing and lending, or that high interest rates reduced loans? When that happens, it implies that there is a negative relationship between interest rate and investment because loans are aimed at investment. This fact explains that there is a direct correlation between interest rate and investment. A high interest rate tends to reduce investment while a low interest rate has an incremental effect on investment.

An example is Mario Draghi who in June 2014 reduced the interest rate for the Euro zone to minus zero one (-0.01) to stimulate banks to lend money to businesses instead of keeping them in the bank. European Central Bank was the first major central bank to apply a negative interest rate. The puzzle then is why Draghi waited this long to apply a negative interest rate while in the United States and Japan, the interest rate was brought down to zero years ago. The fact that Draghi had an available macroeconomic tool to stimulate investment but did not use it all this time raises several issues. The first is that the destiny of our investments is influenced by policymakers. Secondly, it underlines the interdependence and indispensability of man and economic activities, reinforcing my earlier position in this chapter. Finally, it exposes the extent of the delicate condition of our investments as a result of the actions of the policymakers. The reason behind the actions of the policymakers and the effects of their actions will be discussed later.

Let us try to capture in a more practical form the operations and effect of the interest rate on investment with an example. Let us look at a factory owner who is considering investing on solar-powered car. We will presume the only advantage for the choice of a solar car is of cost advantage in comparison to fuel. If the car will cost $5,000 and generates an income of $500 per annum (the saving the solar car will produce in comparison to fuel), this is a return of 10 per cent per annum. Now if the bond yield for the year is 12 per cent the return on the bond for the same amount spent on the solar car will be enough to cover the $500 that will be saved by buying the solar car. Evidently at that point, the choice of the solar loses its attractiveness, but if the bond yield for the year is 8 per cent, the purchase of the solar car becomes a better alternative because the bond will yield $400, which is less than the $500 saving that will accrue from the purchase of the solar car. If the interest rate is 10 per cent, there is a break-even point between the solar car and the bond. At this point the opportunity cost is zero.

At any given point, billions of investments and opportunities depend on interest rates. From the above example, the decision to invest will make reasonable and profitable investment decision at a given interest rate but will not at the other. As the interest rate appreciates, potential investments lose its economic attraction while as the interest rate depreciates the greater potential investment will be justified. We can as well conclude that there is a negative relationship between interest rate and investment. This also leads us to a second conclusion that those whose decision controls interest rates and other macroeconomic variables also have direct influence on our investments. This brings us face to face with the question this book is trying to answer: How safe is our investment? We can as well add, how safe is our investment in the hands of these politicized policymakers?

Expectation: Another factor that influences investment or determine the dimension of investment is expectation. Every investment leads to a modification in the capital stock and therefore brings a change in the future production capacity and output. As expectation changes positively and brings optimism to investment prospects and remuneration, investment grows, but if the expected return on investment diminishes, investment is affected negatively. It is just natural that before investing on an estate one would want to have information on the rents as well before investing in a bond one will be conscious of the yield. The fact that expectation has a direct effect on investment explains how dangerous speculation could be to investment. Again expectations on investment could be modified by policymakers through government policy and rules. And therefore those who can condition or influence expectation has direct implication on the investment.

Speculation: Earlier we discussed speculation but will briefly revisit it to emphasize the extent of damage it can do to investment. We will focus on recent events concerning one of the most prominent countries in Europe. Silvio Berlusconi is probably the most successful Italian businessman to emerge on the Italian political scene in 1994 after winning the parliamentary election of Italy. Berlusconi dominated the political arena until 2013 when he was ousted from power. Berlusconi was accused by Italian Prosecutor of involvement in numerous scandals including sex with a minor that particularly injured his reputation. He was convicted but remained resolute to retaining his office as the prime minister of Italy. The conviction and understanding at the official quarters was that he needed to hang on to power to save himself from going to prison. Nonetheless, Berlusconi's supporters are still following him with religious passion.

Suddenly something happened. To great astonishment, Berlusconi opted out of office. He resigned as prime minister of Italy. But before then, the spread for the Italian government bond called BTP has skyrocketed to somewhere above 500 per cent. By early December 2011 the interest rate of the ten-year government bond had touched 7 per cent, a level at which Ireland, Portugal, and lately Greece sought a bailout from the European Union. What was known to the public then was that Bundesbank of Deutschland suddenly decided to sell off Italian bonds and consequently the market was flooded with them. This action caused a hiccup at the financial quarters and eroded the confidence on Italian economy. As a follow-up of this single action, the Italian spread skyrocketed to an all-time high level that was unacceptable to the market operators and investors and the Italian economy was heading for default. At that point, the Italian debt burden stood at 120 per cent of the GDP.

The government was at a crossroads, and Berlusconi shamefully bowed out of Palazzo Chigi, the official residence of the prime minister. What led to the crisis then was unknown even to the wise and prudent. Today we are treated to a sort of funny tale that shocked everyone. The first is the latest book by Alan Friedman, *Ammazziamo il Gattopardo*, which revealed a sort of conspiracy that led to the ejection of Berlusconi from government quarters.

The second puzzle was the book *Stress Test: Reflections on Financial Crises*, written by Tim Geithner, US president Barak Obama's former finance minister. In it he alleged the conspiracy by some European officials soliciting him to press for the resignation of Berlusconi.

Another conclusion we are tempted to draw is that if a man entrusted with the destiny of the sixth-largest economy in the world is continuously engaged in sex parties and illegal sex with minors, it exposes the extent of decay at official quarters and the moral decadence of people that govern our economy. I cannot imagine the accusations to be false. As compromised as Berlusconi's character may be, it will be an injustice if Berlusconi should be discharged at the end of this unholy saga.

It is now abundantly clear that the unseen fingers of the financial guru Soros compelled the Bundesbank to sell off the Italian bond. Soros speculated on the Italian government's bond. The German central bank panicked and embarked on a sell-off, and the consequences is the analysis I explained above. Soros did it once with the British pound. That Soros could single-handedly plunge Italy into such a terrible difficulty leaves nothing to be cherished but that Italy is that fragile, to the extent of going bankrupt based of the speculation of Soros, explains the delicate state of our investment. The failure of Italy could have plunged the world into an unprecedented global economic and financial crisis because it could have been impossible to salvage Italy. The common opinion in the financial quarters is that Italy is too big to fail and too big to bail considering that the economy of Italy is four times bigger than the economy of Greece, Ireland, and Portugal combined. Once again we ponder, how safe are our investments?

Public policy obviously has a significant implication directly and indirectly on investment. Because public policy directly affects demand for capital and therefore investment, it seeks to condition and influence the cost of capital. Let's briefly look at how this happens.

In every society, governmental entities and authorities promulgate laws, make policies, and allocate resources. This is indisputable fact at all levels of governance and administration. Public policy therefore is a system of laws, regulatory measures, courses of action, and funding priorities concerning a given topic or project promulgated by a governmental entity or its representatives and parastatals (a quasi-governmental organization, corporation, business, or agency).

Individuals and groups constantly try to shape public policy to suit their interest. Interested parties tend to woo government policy to their favour through education, advocacy, and sometimes mobilization of interest groups. Obviously the process and actions adopted by interest groups to achieve their aim of obtaining favour from the powers that might vary from state to state. While in most Western democracies, it is usually done through lobbying by competing interest groups. In less-developed nations, it is more of inducement. Whichever measure is adopted, the objective is usually to win public policy to their favour. The most instrumental aspect of public policy is law. From a general point of view, the law includes particular legislation and more broadly defined provisions of constitutional or international law. There are many ways the law can influence investment regulations and their applications. Sometimes legislation identifies areas in which research grants can be funded and often determines the proportion of funding allocated to various segments. Herein lies the reason for public debate on policy over proposed legislation and funding.

We shall define advocacy as an attempt to influence public policy and rules through campaign, education, lobbying, or political pressure. Advocacy groups often attempt to educate the masses, as well as public policymakers, about the nature of problems. Often they propose the legislation needed to address the problems, and the funding necessary to offer services or conduct research. Despite individual and general opinions on advocacy even at the professional and research community, it is clear that public policy priorities are influenced by advocacy. Sound research data, information, and professional guidance can be used to educate the public as well as policymakers, thereby improving the public policy procedure and outcome. Unfortunately, the reverse is the case in most situations because of political gains, and that is what puts our investment in jeopardy.

Despite the influence of advocacy on policymakers, knowledge and empirical evidence has shown that politicians ponder on projects, policies, and programs with immediate returns. But before we delve into this aspect of a 'fire-brigade approach' of politicians' policy issues, let's see some of the policies that will help us understand importance of political influence on our investment.

Repatriation of foreign earning: Again, let us start with the United States as an example. As a consequence of high corporate tax, foreign-based US companies usually keep their earnings in their subsidiary companies rather than repatriating it to the United States. The same is applicable to most other European and North American companies. The US marginal tax tends to be the highest in the developed world, and this has led to billions in foreign earnings being frozen in the so-called financial safe havens. Let's precisely state that among these funds are those that purposely sneaked their illegally accumulated wealth to foreign countries to evade paying taxes. The Italian Mafia and the Chinese are clear examples of these funds. Corrupt politicians are excluded from these groups. Although a Democratic president (because Democrats are not known for monetary contraction through tax cuts but for monetary expansion) President Obama, in his 2012 State of the Union Address, proposed creating a 'minimum tax' on foreign earnings of US multinationals as a way of curbing or at least reducing resistance to repatriation of foreign earnings. The tax is designed to guarantee that all foreign profits of US multinationals are taxed once at a minimum rate, either by the United States, the host country, or another country.

Recently some members of the parliament belonging to both parties (Republicans and Democrats) called for a tax break on repatriated earning. Members were proposing tax cuts similar to the one implemented in 2004 during the George Bush administration when taxes were reduced to an all-time low of 5.25 per cent on repatriated funds. The government of Silvio Berlusconi of Italy embarked on repatriation of funds during his tenure. Between 2001 and 2009, Berlusconi declared amnesty on repatriated funds three times. Investors who repatriated their earnings using those amnesty wavers paid as low as 5 per cent tax on repatriated funds.

Level of economic activity: Another factor that influences investments and investment decisions is the level of economic activity. When there is a boom on the level of production, investment is boosted. This is because an increment in production level leads to an increase on the demand for capital, thereby increasing investment. Also, the level of economic activity increases the GDP, thereby positively affecting investment. As we have discussed earlier, the increase in the GDP usually has a multiplier effect because it leads to an increase in aggregate demand, which in return increases household income, leading to greater consumption, and greater consumption leads to further aggregate demand, and consequently an additional increase in investment. Policymakers have a tool in their hands to control GDP. Monetary expansion and contraction have direct implications on GDP and impacts investment as a result. The eighty-euro bonus awarded by the Italian government under Matteo Renzi is a classical example. The 'Udoji Award' (Chief Jerome Udorji was appointed by the federal government of Nigeria under Yakubu Gowon to draw a development program for Nigeria. Udorji as the head of the civil service compensation and review committee suggested salary increase and compensation for the civil servant. The compensation and salary increases are known today as Udoji Award) adopted by the Nigerian government under Gowon's administration is another fatal economic blunder of monetary expansion.

Another of such example is the policy initiative taken by the Kennedy administration in the 1960s. The policy had a significant effect on the demand for capital because it sought to affect the cost of capital for firms. President Kennedy, on assumption of office, introduced two such strategies. The first method accelerated depreciation gave firms the opportunity to depreciate capital assets over a very short period of time. This gave firms the right to report artificially high production costs in the first years of an asset's life and thus report lower profits and pay less tax. It is worthy to note that accelerated depreciation did not seek to change the actual rate at which assets depreciated, but it reduced tax payments during the early years of the asset's use and thus lowered the cost of holding capital.

The second method was the investment tax credit that allowed a firm to reduce its tax liability by a percentage of its investment within a given period. A firm acquiring new capital is permitted to subtract part of its cost from the taxes it owed the government. During the Kennedy administration, the amount of tax cut permitted was 10 per cent. In reality, the government assumed the responsibility of paying 10 per cent of the cost of any new capital; the investment tax credit thus reduced the cost of capital for firms. In this way, Kennedy was able to boost investment, therefore creating a positive investment condition, at least for people. However, we are concerned with the propensity with which Kennedy was able to impact investment.

We have briefly discussed a few methods in which policymakers can directly or indirectly influence investments and investment decisions. There are numerous others, including tax reduction or increase on corporate profits and capital gains. Policymakers can also apply accelerated depreciation or investment tax credit. All these measures have a direct impact on investment and are ready tools in the hand of politicians who are directly or indirectly the policymakers. Were investments decisions left only to market forces and economic variables and activities, this work could not have made an academic sense, but after a critical analysis of the environments under which our investments exist, it was blatantly clear that at the root of the forces governing our project and investments is political might.

The aim of this part of the book is to explore the interrelatedness of investment failure and the human factor. I will expose these grey areas later. In the meantime, let's try to understand how these politicians achieve power.

After a long search for a political ideology and evolution, mankind settled for democracy as the most viable form of governance. The theme of this book is not the merits or demerits of democracy, nor are we concerned with the alternatives to democracy or the comparison of democracy with other political systems. The major concern of this work is to access the implications of politics on investment with special attention to investment failure.

Democracy deals with political or social equality. Suffice it to say a state characterized by formal equality of rights and privileges is considered a democratic state. In a democratic setup, citizens choose their leaders by vote. Democracy strives to enshrine the supremacy of the people's freedom to exercise their right. It encompasses social, religious, cultural, ethnic, and racial equality, justice, and liberty. Let us formally define democracy as a form of government in which the supreme and ultimate power is entrusted in the electorate and exercised by them directly or indirectly through a system of representation usually involving periodically held free elections. Put another way, democracy is the government of the people, by the people, and for the people. In a democracy, power is exercised by the people directly or through their agents and representatives. This definition emphasizes the supremacy of the people. If the people are supreme, then their numerical strength counts. Herein lies the obvious fact that democracy is a game of number, and herein lies the drama we are trying to unravel. Is democracy really a blessing to mankind? Norman Mailer once said, "Democracy is the noblest form of government we have yet evolved". Mailer is not alone in this position because it is a generally held conception. To what extent is this affirmation true? Before we go into that, let's take a step further to see how democracy metamorphosed.

It is necessary to draw a line at this juncture concerning certain consolidated notions regarding democracy. The issue of eligibility questions the notion of freedom. As well, the issue of adult suffrage or universal adult suffrage places an embargo on some people to exercise their voting right. If all humans really are equal before the law, then all humans should be free to vote and be voted for. If for any reason certain people cannot vote or be voted for, even when the reason for the prohibition is rooted or prescribed by the law, democracy loses its meaning of universality. However, I have come to realise that freedom is not free anywhere on earth but has to be fought for and conquered by the interested people.

Democracy (written as *demokratia* in Greek) means 'rule of the people'. Demokratia was founded from *demos*, meaning 'people' while *kratos* means 'power' or 'rule'. The political system existing in classical Athens then granted democratic citizenship and participation to a class of elite among the free men while excluding slaves and women from political participation. In virtually all democratic governments throughout history, democratic citizenship consisted of an elite class until full enfranchisement was conquered for all adult citizens in most modern democracies through the suffrage movements of the nineteenth and twentieth centuries.

There exits several forms of democracy, among which are two basic forms, both of which deal with how the whole body of all eligible citizens executes its will. The major and most popular form of democracy is direct democracy, in which all eligible citizens have direct and active participation in the political decision making. In most modern democracies, which we are mostly concerned with in this work, the whole body of all eligible citizens remains the sovereign power, but political power is exercised indirectly through elected representatives. This is what is mostly referred to as representative democracy while states that operate this model of political system are regarded as democratic republic. The concept of representative democracy arose largely from ideas and institutions that developed during the European Middle Ages going through the reformation and the enlightenment period extending to the French and American revolutions.

Aristotle said, "One factor of liberty is to govern and be governed in turn; for the popular principle of justice is to have equality according to number, not worth". This is already an accepted and established concept among scholars, but that is my major disagreement with democracy. The problem with most of these ancient theories is that these men lived in a different era and environment, where there existed a different social setting, a different cultural orientation, a different ethical concept. One may be surprised to hear that until the evolution of the Protestants, the Roman Catholic Church, the dominant or only existing Christian church, preached against profit-making in business. Those were the days of the Italian Renaissance. The Protestant teachers and leaders integrated the spiritual and temporary life. Far from extolling the life of poverty and spiritual contemplation as separate from worldly life, Protestants preached that it was pious to make the most use of one's God-given talents in daily business and commercial activities. This partly explains why the evolution of economics and market delayed until the 1700s. These are part of the issues that those who advocate Keynes's method in modern economics do not take into consideration. However, Keynes's theory has been sufficiently treated earlier in this book and will not be revisited here.

The major constraint of democracy is that it shifted the policy, decision, control, and administration of our investments and resources to the less educated – the peasant, the pauper, and the less informed because since they are the majority in every society or democracy, and democracy, as we know, is a numbers game that conveniently determines who goes into power. The power to decide what happens to our investments then is with them. The fact that our investments are in the hands of 'commoners' makes them prone to manipulation, apparently because this class of the people can be easily manipulated.

The commoners usually do not have all the required education and information necessary to analyze the promises and in some cases the program of whomever comes to seek their vote. Consequently, their lack of adequate information and their poor economic condition leaves them open to manipulation. More often than not, the election program and manifestos are too sophisticated and technical for the elites to read and comprehend, never mind the commoners. Sometimes the programs are too voluminous and often demand expertise to comprehend. Politicians themselves know the commoners lack the technical capacity to comprehend their projects and therefore play on their intelligence. There are situations where votes are bargained and sold to the highest bidder. There is evidence of block votes being sold to politicians in southern parts of Italy, such as Napoli and Palermo.

In Africa, South America, and Asia, the situation is nothing to write home about. In places like Nigeria a vote could be bought for any price. A bag of rice is enough to win a family vote. Most often in Africa people do not know the name of the candidate they are voting for in an election. In Nigeria people will tell the politicians that they are not interested in your programs because they are going into power to enrich themselves therefore all the want is their own share of the cake. Where there are no monetary inducements there are other forms of inducements. Inducement could take the form of vain promises or unrealizable projects. In places like North America inducement takes mostly the form promises.

Obama had to promise health-care reform and green energy to get elected to the white house. On assumption of office he made frantic efforts to fulfil the election promise of reforming health care, even to the detriment of American interest. Yes I say at the detriment of American interest for I consider it an act of financial irresponsibility and recklessness by Obama administration to embark on health-care reform at the comatose condition Obama met the American economy. Health-care reform as Obama wanted it will only aggravate the already-aggravated financial condition of America and swell the American debt even more. Reagan promised the liberation of American hostages held in Iran to secure power. That was a dangerous game that ended positively. The point we are trying to make is that Obama went ahead with his program of health-care reform to make political gains, and not for economic reasons. That explains how risky and dangerous our investment could be in the hands of politicians. As we have said earlier, man is conceited in nature and that explains the giving of vote to Obama on the promise of health-care reform.

A recent case is the election of the European Union that was just concluded. Some European politicians manipulated the masses using the current economic hardship the world is going through. There exists a political party in Italy called Lega Nord, which was formed about two decade ago to fight for the secession of northern Italy from the rest of the country. As usual with Italian political parties, after a few glorious years the party fell into financial scandal that consumed founder Umberto Bossi. As a last resort, the party passed the leadership baton, and finally Matteo Salvini came onboard. Salvini spent the campaign period shouting that Italy will pull out of the European currency (the euro). This single message, with his proposal of an embargo on immigration, catapulted Lega from 2 per cent to 6.3 per cent within a three-month period. Despite the financial and economic implications of pulling out of the euro zone, it will spell doom for Italy, considering its high national debt burden.

Salvini cannot even initiate the process of pulling Italy out of euro currency, firstly because Lega does not have the numerical strength in the parliament, and secondly because he is not part of the coalition government in Italy. Lega does not belong to the coalition that will form the new European government. It is therefore clear even to Salvini that he can never fulfil those election promises. Salvini said what the electorate wanted to hear, and they gave him their vote. Were the electorate that naïve to see through these vain promises, or at least understand that Lega does not have the power to fulfil these promises? Especially when they were part of the coalition that plunged Italy into the economic disaster it is going through during the twelve years they governed Italy. The important thing to note is how our leaders are selected, and these leaders are the ones saddled with the management of our economy and therefore our investment.

Another political miracle of the last EU election was Nigel Farage and Marine Le Pen. Farage has been the leader of UK Independence Party UKIP since 2010. Marie Le Pen, the youngest daughter of the long-time leader of Front National, the far right of France, succeeded his father as the leader of the extreme right party, FN. Both Farage and Le Pen were able to take their parties to the first position in the last EU election in their respective countries. While Farage UKIP became the first party in the United Kingdom, Le Pen's party became the first in France, relegating the ruling party to the third position.

Anybody who listens to these two people in their public discussion knows they have something in common. Both are against immigration. That these politicians gained their votes, especially because they coined slogans against immigration, tells the mind-sets of the electorate. It explains how myopic and shrewd the electorate can be.

Other opportunists still exist. Grillo, the Italian comedian-turned-politician, belongs to this group. Geert Wilders also leads the Populist Party in Germany, currently the fourth party in Germany. Hyder, the Austrian politician, had come and gone. All these opportunistic bourgeoisie manipulated the electorate for their personal interest and that of their political party, for they know the impossibility of achieving what they proposed during their campaign. That a comedian like Grillo, who had no political, administrative, or professional training of any form could become the first party in his first adventure into politics is enough food for thought. These men, like every other politician, had a project (some are sometimes secret projects). They usually fool the electorate to achieve their project, and by virtue of that political victory will inherit the management of the administration or government and therefore our investment. One is tempted to ask once again, but in a different dimension, how safe is our investment in the hands of these men?

If democracy was the best form of selecting leaders, we should have had the best people in government and the most competent hands to manage our organizations and investment. Unfortunately, in many cases the reverse is true. Sadly, democracy has not guaranteed decency in our institutions. In sharp contrast, the best managed and most vibrant institutions are the undemocratic ones. The International Monetary Fund (IMF) and EU central bank are a few examples. The major error in the constitution of the European Union project was of putting the cart before the horse. The EU is a wonderful idea that should have started with a political union before getting to an economic and a social amalgamation. The lack of political unity is the major constraint to a formidable EU. From the beginning of the global crisis, the EU has found it almost impossible to find a common front to handle the drastic crisis. The haphazard handling of the Greek crisis attests to this fact.

Despite the magnanimous economic power of the EU, it has little or minimum influence on global and international politics. France and the United Kingdom, who are both members of the EU, flagrantly disregarded the EU to attack Libya during the 2011 upsurge in North Africa. That attempt to forcefully install democracy not only failed in Libya but also in Egypt and Iraq. These countries were better off without the importation of democracy from the so-called developed world. The most recent was the 2014 crisis in the Ukraine, where the United States and Russia entered into a dialogue about the way forward. They did this without inviting the EU, who are the Ukraine's closest neighbours.

As the economic and financial crisis lingers, the only European institution that has performed marvellously well is the European central bank. Under Mario Draghi, it was able to take certain initiatives to combat the crisis. To stimulate investment, Draghi reduced the interest rate to zero. He lent about 200 billion euro to banks to stimulate lending to desiring organizations and institutions. Draghi guaranteed the national debt of the component European nations to salvage their anaemic economies from collapsing. This single decision salvaged countries like Italy and Spain and brought down the spread on their individual national debts to below 150 per cent.

Fortunately and unfortunately, the European Central Bank is not a democratic institution. The president, like the president of the European Union, is not appointed by the ignorant masses. The tenure is a non-renewable eight years and therefore is shielded from the politicking in the European Union. The president is appointed by the consensus of the majority of the eighteen-member euro financial zones.

The president of the World Bank, Jim Yong Kim, as well as the president of the IMF, Christine Lagarde, are appointed by the consensus of the member states. From their inception, these two important financial bodies have been headed by the United States and Europe. While the World Bank has been always headed by the United States, the IMF has been headed by a European. Despite the fact that the leadership of these two powerful institutions have always been a product of selective bargaining, they have always had some of the best brainpower the world can offer. These institutions represent excellence in administration and resourcefulness in financial output. They are objective and productive despite a few lapses (which do not fall under the purview of this book).

The underlying argument is that despite the gridlock that comes with the democratic process, if the leaders of the world best and most important financial institutions do not attain office through a popular vote, democracy then may not be the best alternative, at least in financial circles. Even the UN secretary general does not emerge through a popular vote by election but by a mechanism that could be likened to consensus (or more or less a veto). However, electing the UN secretary general through a popular vote may be a complex and impossible notion. My conclusion is that one of the greatest threats confronting our investment is democracy. It is not wrong to suggest that our investments are safer in the hands of competent and seasoned professional whose ascension to position and office are devoid of political manoeuvres and intrigue.

So far we have made a case in favour of the excellent performance of the undemocratically elected leadership in most of the world's most important financial institutions. Some of the world's most corrupt and incompetent leaders are democratically elected. The major problem with democracy is that it creates alliances and sometimes administrative gridlock. Since nobody can get to power democratically without lobbying, alliances, bargaining, and more often than not impossible promises, democratic offices are flawed from the beginning. Political office holders should be selected by a team of independent professional and should serve a single tenure enough to conclude their program. Machiavelli said that those who attain power with an alien force will have to be obedient to the army that brought them into power, or destroy the army that brought them into power and build a new one.

The reason behind this argument is that survival of every leader mostly depends on peaceful coexistence between them and those who brought them into power. Experience has shown that except in rare occasions, those in the corridors of power are more powerful than those in the seat of power. Evidence abounds that, except the politicians are loyal to those who brought them into power – or they should be able to build an army strong enough to eliminate the power that brought them into office – they may not know peace. The current ordeal of the president of the federal Republic of Nigeria Goodluck Jonathan is a clear example of a failed attempt to change the powers that be and how dangerous such attempts might be. The Boko Haram insurgents in Nigeria attest to this fact. Goodluck is a product of selective bargaining and part of the bargain is that he will not run a second time. He reneged on this understanding and his opponents decided to make Nigeria ungovernable for him. Nigeria has lost thousands of lives and billions of dollars to the horrific activities of the sect since the insurgency intensified under Jonathan administration.

One of the major problem confronting investments is democracy. A major fallout of democracy is that most of our organizations and investments are governed by mediocrity. This is because politicians make rules that govern investments and appoint those that chair the organizations and parastatals. This correlation between investment and politics greatly conditions investment because even in some critical situations, investment decisions depend on political ties and not on return on investment (ROI). Because of political ties and commitments, policymakers are compelled to satisfy their agents and cronies before delving into the interest of the organization. Those who are already in power will have to lobby and satisfy their paymasters to maintain their positions. Politically ordained managers usually have preferential treatment and access to subsidy and assistance. Managers and directors of important and strategic organizations most often than not are appointed based on political ties and affiliations and not on merit or professional competence.

As a result of political manoeuvres, most strategic organizations and, therefore, investments, are managed by lawyers and engineers and not trained managers. Management is an art but also a science, so for institutions and investments to get the proper and adequate attention, investments should be handled by professionally trained managers. Management scholars obviously understand the significance of this argument. I have never seen, for example, an engineer in the courtroom or a lawyer in a laboratory. We therefore have to change our thinking and understand that management is not a profession for every Tom, Dick, and Harry. A major start toward protecting our investments is to leave our organizations in the hands of trained and professional managers.

Inasmuch as I understand the arguments in favour of succession from within, it should happen only when the successors have acquired professional training necessary to take over the management of the organizations, especially strategic organizations. It is true that succession from within sometimes motivates and guarantees dedication and commitment, but strategic reasoning and innovation should not always be sacrificed for dynasty. The argument that some unprofessional managers have succeeded in management positions does not hold water because there is no yard stick to measure what should have happened if they were professionally trained or if those position at that specific time were taken over by professionals or management gurus.

Only trained managers are strategically competent to take organizations to the next level and sometimes the outer space. Organization must continuously change and innovate. Change must be managed, and only professionals understand this chemistry. Successful management of our investments and their future depend on visionary leaders. The debate in many quarters that managers' salaries and fringe benefits are too high shows how naïve people at the helm of affairs are towards management. I don't know of any country where it is a crime to be rich even in the communist states. What is democratic about pegging the price of managers below the actual market value? Does that not violate the free market economy we are clamouring for? If the world is truly free and all humans are equal before the law then nobody should compel the other to earn less than the monetary worth of the rendered services. Government intervention in a free market should be discouraged even in this situation. Management as an art has no limit to creation. Creativity is a rare skill and therefore can not be measured. Charisma is a special quality found in a privileged few. Although management skill can be learned it has its hurdle. The successful blending of these qualities make a level 5 leader. A quintessential leader is rare to find and can not be measured.

Because we cannot separate investment or organizations from change, let's take a few steps forward to explain exactly what management stands for. This step will help show why professional managers are instrumental to successful investment. We will also try to understand whether management is an art or a science, especially where the conception among those who assume management positions without formal training believe management is an art.

Management: An Art or a Science?

We shall take a scholarly and practical approach to this question. Let me first reaffirm that studying history does not mean merely arranging events in chronological other; it involves developing an understanding of the impact of societal forces on organizations, as Richard Daft (an American organizational theorist and professor of management at Vanderbilt University) suggested. He went further to say that studying history is a way to achieve strategic thinking, to see the big picture, and to improve conceptual skills. Generally it is recognised that management as a concept is a wide-ranging subject. Contributions from a variety of disciplines have left their mark on the development of modern management thought. This means the study of management cannot be undertaken entirely in terms of a single discipline.

It will be necessary to provide a multidisciplinary approach to this study. Let me also say that by multidisciplinary, I mean behavioural and social sciences. *Behavioural sciences deal with the behaviour of people.* In some quarters, all the major five subjects – anthropology, sociology, psychology, economics, and political science – that influence management are considered behavioural science, but in others, behavioural science is taken strictly to apply to only three of them namely anthropology, sociology and psychology. We will consider the influence of each of these discipline one after the other before we draw our conclusion.

Anthropology is concerned with the science of mankind and the study of human behaviour as a whole. As far as organizational behaviour and management is concerned, the main focus of attention is on the cultural system, beliefs, customs, ideas, and values within a group or society and the comparison of behaviour among different cultures. Two of the main anthropological contributions are in the area of organizational culture and in providing useful methodological tools for management. Some of these contributions are developing an understanding of behavioural patterns; and social groupings, rituals, symbols, and languages within the organization or within a particular group of employees. Examples of anthropologists who contributed to the study of management are Mouly and Sankaran, who studied research and development departments in Indian organizations.

Sociology is concerned with the study of social behaviour, relationships among social groups and societies, its origin, and the maintenance of order. The main focus is on the analysis of social structures and positions in those structures. The main relationship between sociology and management are in the areas of how people interact; the effects of different organizational structures on people; and the ways in which business and management have impacted a wider society. Sociology has particularly contributed to our understanding of social relations within the organization, such as in the interaction of employees, power relations, and social groups.

Another central issue for sociology is the study of social change. Sociologists view business organizations as socially constructed. They do not see organizations as natural but that they exist as a result of the effort of people and because *people* decide to recognise they exist. Sociologists who contributed to management include Emile Durkheim, who was interested in the division of labour; and Max Weber, a theorist whose contribution to management was on the understanding of structures, hierarchies, and authority within organization. Karl Marx provided a theory of social life based on the social relations of production. Marx was against the dominant pattern for organizing production and called for it to be overthrown.

Psychology is concerned with the study of human behaviour, with traits of the individual and membership of small social groups. The main focus of attention is on the individual as a whole, or what is called the personality system, including perceptions, attitudes, and motives. The processes that are studied are those seen to be determined by the inner mechanisms of the mind and include the processes of perception, memory, and learning. Prominent contributions include the works of Hertzberg, Maslow, and Vroom. Such noble contributions include psychological contract, which means the unwritten agreement of what the organization and the employee will both give and receive. This concept arose as a result of the recognition that not all expectations were or could be formalized in the legal contract of employment. This approach is related to motivation but more specifically to both the organization and the employee. Another vital contribution of psychology is the work group. Work group are of interest to psychologists because they consist of a number of people who are psychologically aware of each other, who interact with each other, and who perceive themselves to be a group for a particular purpose.

Economics is concerned with understanding the mechanism for the allocation of limited resources to achieve unlimited wants. One of the major economic contributions to management is the focus on those management activities that are related to profit maximization. This assumes that the overall mission of the organization is ultimately to create as much profit as possible, for as long as possible. This will remain the guiding principle for all decisions made by managers at all levels of the organization.

Economic contributions to management were made by Douma and Schreuder in their book, which said economic approaches to organizations are fruitful whenever the problems to be studied have an economic aspect (Douma and Schreuder, 1998, p. 4)– that is to say whenever part of the problem deals with the problem of the allocation of scarce resources. Other contributions are in behavioural theory (under this concept, economics see organization as made up of different participants who each have their own interest), agency theory, transaction cost economics, economic approaches to strategic management, etc.

Political science deals with power because the science of politics deals with the strategy for the evolution of power to control people. Political forces refer to the influence of political and legal institutions on people and organizations. The relation of political science to management concerns the control of complex organizations. Political science also made numerous contributions in the study of leadership and power sharing in management. Other disciplines such as mathematics, biology, engineering, and information science also contributed in numerous ways to management. Just remember the work of Fredrick Taylor the American mathematician who invented scientific management.

*

The role of manager and the skills needed for the position were discussed in the previous chapter. For a manager to be successful, he or she needs to have *human and conceptual skills*. Leadership also require *charismatic traits or qualities to succeed*. These characteristics, including the ones mentioned above cannot be studied or imparted from a textbook. We all are witnesses of such statements as, 'Leaders are born, not made!' However, these sterling qualities are not enough for a successful management career. Management is also a science, a multidisciplinary science, as we have discussed earlier, because a growing body of knowledge and objective facts describes management and how to attain organizational performance. The knowledge is acquired through systematic research and can be conveyed through teaching and textbooks. Becoming a successful manager requires a blend of formal learning and practice of science and art. *Therefore, management is both science and art.*

The emphasis is to reinforce the fact that management is not only art but a science and therefore should be learned for proper administration of management principles, skills, and techniques. Democracy has robbed organizations the possibility of having professionals and competent managers in position of management in organization, public institutions, and parastatal. In most situations, managers ascend to their position, and in other cases they are anointed by political leaders. Sometimes access to classified information is the exclusive reserve and privilege of politically connected managers, thereby making a case for politically anointed managers. A vicious circle that is deeply rooted to the electorate since it is the electorate that determines who ascends to which office. For those who are voted into power decides who the policymakers should be.

The policymaker makes rules for organizations and institutions and decides who takes which office. The electorates are not always rational in their voting decisions. Sometimes they don't have the right information or are unable to analyze the projects and programs proposed by the politicians. In most situations their heart rules their brain. Most voting decisions are irrational because they were made out of sentiment. Winners are not always those who have good projects and programs for the community but those whose ovation were loudest at a given moment. Those who get into power therefore do not bother to do what is right but appease those who brought them into power, as there returning to power does not depend on their legacy.

An electorate costs less than a bag of rice. The poverty of the mind-set of the electorate spells doom for investment. As far as the majority of the electorates are the poor and the peasants there is no clear exit from the turbulent and murky water investment is continuously treading.

So far we have shown that democracy is at the root of investment failure because it made the weaker part of society, and therefore the ignorant masses who can be easily manipulated by the rich and powerful the king makers. Adam Smith saw it coming many years ago and concluded by saying, "The real tragedy of the poor is the poverty of their aspirations".

Who Might Pay These Debts?

The national debt figure of the world's largest economy the United States of America as at 23 of June 2014 stood at a record $17,606,516,662,573. In 2011, when we started this book, the debt figure was fourteen trillion dollars, while in 2012 it stood at sixteen trillion. The aim is not to bother the reader with figures but to establish one obvious fact: that our investment is continuously threatened because of the increasingly monstrous debt figure of most countries.

The GDP of the United States presently stands at $16.8 trillion dollars, and the debt share of every American citizen is a whooping $55,257. The one million-dollar question then is, who might pay this debt? Although we have used the United States as a yard stick for our argument, the situation is not better for other developed nations.

The Italian debt figure stands at $2.12 trillion while the GDP stands at $1.569 trillion. The estimated growth rate is 1 per cent, which seems unrealizable, at least for now. The share of the national debt per citizen stands at 34,802 euro. The percentage of the Italian debt to GDP is 127 per cent. Japan's national debt stands at 1,017 trillion yen while the share for each citizen remains 8,000.373 yen. The percentage of Japanese debt to GDP is 197.25 per cent. Except for Germany and China, whose debt ratio to their GDP stands at a level far below 100 per cent, the rest of the world's major economies are struggling with national debt figures close to 100 per cent of their national income. The total debt for the world economy stands at $58,847 trillion.

After the Great Recession, when the US economy soared to an all-time high of 12 per cent to the GDP, the debt started decreasing from since the time of President Truman. The Carter regime saw the debt decrease to 30 per cent, but after his administration, the debt continued its upward trend. From the Reagan administration, the US debt increased, with a mild decline during the Clinton administration. The Obama administration twice risked default.

Although the world debt is a vicious circle because of the interconnectedness of the world economy, especially in view of the globalization, the basic argument is that the world debt has continued to appreciate. As the dynamics and mechanism of accumulating debt does not fall under the aim of this work our concern is the implication of the increasing world debt for investment.

The presumption is that the debt will be paid when the national or world economy regains growth, but the question is, at what rate will the world economy grow to meet the repayment of these debts considering the innumerable debt burden that has to be born in form of servicing debt interest? In view of the rate of the debt to GDP, will the economy ever grow enough to pay these debts? Will a nation ever sacrifice all that accrued through growth to repayment of debt? What happens to infrastructural development, research, and technology if a nation invests all its earnings in repayment of debt?

Although it is not feasible, but even at that how many years will it take a nation to pay the debt considering that the debt of some nations is above 100 per cent, and the growth rate is below 2 per cent? If there will ever be enough growth rate to repay the debt, when will that be in view of the fact that the debt has continuously increased? Evidently, the debt has continued to increase because the world has continued to spend more than it earns.

This is our argument against the proponents of Keynes's theory as a solution to the current economic crisis. We need to remind ourselves that the world debt has continuously appreciated because of overspending. When will this trend end? The present generation lacks the moral conviction to confront the reality of our existence. We simply cannot continue to spend more than we earn.

The moral obligation staring this generation in the face is the will to make the appropriate sacrifice to return the world economy to the path of growth through sanitizing the economy. If the present generation refuses to make the appropriate sacrifice to reduce the world debt, what moral justification do we have to presume that, the succeeding generations will make the sacrifice that we, the actual culprits of this heinous crime, have refused to make? What's good for the goose should be good for the gander. The world leaders, as we have established in the previous chapters, have refused to apply the corrective macroeconomic measures to sanitize the world economy because of the consequences and political inconvenience that comes with austerity measures.

Helmut Kohl adopted macroeconomic measures in the form of reform to correct the German economy, and he lost the election. Although Kohl lost out on the political game, his corrective reforms returned Germany to the path of growth and created the foundation for the robust economic growth that Germany has enjoyed. This was instrumental to the dynamism and ease with which Germany has managed the current economic crisis.

Mario Monti also paid a political price for the adoption of the reforms that salvaged Italy from the economic disaster his country was facing at the exit of Berlusconi. Italy was salvaged from an imminent economic default, but Monti was almost humiliated out of office in the election that followed. The fact that Gianfranco Fini did not return to the Italian parliament and Pier Ferdinando Casini won about two per cent vote in the last Italian political election in 2013 explains there is something wrong with the electorate.

Unfortunately, there is no justification for failure. These men rooted for reform and paid the imminent political price. Nothing hurts like suffering in isolation for being patriotic.

These examples are enough evidence to reiterates our position that politicians shy away from corrective economic reform and reinforce the fact that electorates are more often than not irrational in the voting booth. This has continued and will continue to create a non-conducive environment for economic and investment growth.

AFTERWORD

Analysis

The author has described and analyzed the circumstances and factors surrounding the failure of investment and its consequences.

Conclusion

This work has tried to address the causes of financial crisis, investment failure, and its eventual consequences. To some extent, investment failure cannot be completely eliminated, especially when investment is naturally associated with a degree of risk. If there were no risk, there would be no investments. There is a consensus among scholars and financial operators that economic retardation and decline follows growth. The conclusion, therefore, is that as investment failure cannot be completely eradicated from the system, it could be reduced or at worst controlled.

However, the aim of every investor is to make a profit, and the aim of most studies has been to avoid or at least reduce the risk associated with investment. Theories like portfolio diversification and investment theory were aimed at addressing such issues. The current financial crisis has undoubtedly exposed the weaknesses of the policymakers in addressing the problem. It also revealed the unpreparedness of the public and private operators for such eventual situation considering that the world had experienced series of crisis in the past. Although democracy is seen and accepted as the best political option and form of government at least at the moment, this book has tried hard to explain that democracy played a pivotal role in the failure of investment. This is because one of the fundamental reasons for the failure of investment is bad governmental policies. However, each financial crisis always comes in a different dimension and with a different effect.

Evidently, the current crisis started in the United States but extended to the rest of the world because of a lack of effective containment measures in place to combat such situations. A lesson to learn and adopt as a curative measure for future occurrences is that efficient crisis containment requires a clear allocation of responsibilities with explicit objectives and powers, proper channels of accountability, and more transparency. Furthermore, the book is advocating for a model of governance framework, at the core of which should be a crisis-containment council.

Specifically at the onset of the current crisis, the world was lost as to who does what. Confronted with such unprecedented financial turmoil, the government was forced to step in to save the financial system from inevitable collapse. The confusion remained on how the government actions should work and who should be responsible. The memorandum of understanding between the government agents, supervisory authorities, and central banks were simply not able to distribute the share of crisis responsibilities. Also, the government and central bank interventions were insufficient, or in certain situations non-existent. Therefore the crisis degenerated.

After extensive review and study of several failed investments and governmental policies in place, the author noted that part of the difficulty of the financial sector is a general acceptable accounting standard. The world financial community would be better off with a minimum consensus on developing and enforcing a working standard for accountants and making them accountable and responsible for their accounting reports, especially in view of the globalisation and its eventual prospects.

The assumption of responsibility will make them pay greater attention to the documents received for preparing accounting reports. The lack of policy and poor application of soft laws partly brought us to where we are today. At least the application of the Basel I and II accords should be a good start. Also, greediness by institutional and private investors for high ROIs played a significant role in triggering the crisis. It is the greediness in all of us, who were taking it for granted that a return of a well-above-average interest rate was the norm that brought us to where we are.

The housing bubble burst, and the credit card racket and trading of asset-backed securities as secured bonds are sure proof of the greediness of financial institutions and investors alike. The trading of hedge funds and derivatives caused severe damage to the world economy, and the demand for their serious regularization is not misplaced. It calls for an international valid supervisory system to arrest these issues.

Going forward, the policymakers still have a lot to do in assuring investors of the security of their investment. This will help in restoring the confidence of the investors and return the world to growth. Proper macroeconomic principles should be adopted by the authorities to correct the impending danger that looms as a result of large deficits and overspending. It demands courage, and the time to start is now. The future economic growth will depend on the way monetary and fiscal policies continue to respond to the general and long-lasting degradation of the state of affairs.

Investors have a duty to invest more in the stabilization and normalization of the political environment. This should come in the form of an enlightenment campaign and education of the electorate. Ethics and values should be given more attention and inculcated into the body politic. As far as the majority of the world population remains illiterate and poor, the possibility of selecting the appropriate people to lead our institutions and subsequently the organizations will remain a mirage. Efforts should be directed towards a single tenure of a minimum of six years and a maximum of eight to ensure stability. This is because every political change comes with realignment of political order and policy that usually causes a hiccup in the investment program and prospect. The world should start thinking of a better way of selecting their leaders. A situation where political officers are selected by a few independent professionals will not be out of order. Devolution of powers should be adopted to make political offices less attractive.

This is where to start. Unfortunately, this generation has demonstrated that they lack the moral conscience to do what is right to remedy the impasse the world economy is been subjected to. The youth has a duty to join me in this mass enlightenment campaign (start by asking the person nearest to you, 'Who Might Pay These Debt'). The damage and decay done to the economy is so insidious that only a radical and drastic action can return the world to proper growth. The world is not ready for another revolution or at least a generational shift. The world is too comfortable and obsessed with their wealth to embark on a probable endless adventure. We are spoilt and so pampered that we are unable to make a sacrifice no matter how little. The next generation will then have to pay dearly for our inactions and this erroneous abdication of responsibility. Wole Soyinka[9] said "We have lost the twentieth century are we still bent on loosing the twenty-first century?" History will not forgive us for such a wilful sin of omission.

The political class needs more competent and professional people. Those who say they are not interested in politics allow themselves to be led and governed by their inferiors. The obvious truth is that not only our investments but even our destiny is in the hands of the political class that are the policymakers. All hands therefore should be on deck to leave a bequeathing legacy for the succeeding generation. This is where we stand.

---

[9] Wole Soyinka a noble Laureate is a professor of literature at Obafemy Awolowo University Nigeria).

GLOSSARY

Capitalist Economy An economic system that emphasizes a free market without government intervention. Usually in a capitalist economy the government will intervene only to protect private ownership. "A system of economics based on the private ownership of capital and production inputs, and on the production of goods and services for profit. The production of goods and services is based on supply and demand in the general market (market economy), rather than through central planning (planned economy). Capitalism is generally characterized by competition between producers". http://www.investopedia.com/terms/c/capitalism.asp

Collateralized Debt Obligation (CDO) The CDO is a collection of different types of credit and risk, often referred to as slices or tranches. CDO security is uniquely structured in a way where each slice has a different date of maturity and risk. The higher rate the CDO pays, the higher the risk. This is because the CDO is divided into different risk tranches, whereby senior tranches are considered more secure than junior tranches.

Collectivism A principle or philosophy either political economical or social that gives preference or emphasizes the interdependence of human over individual. "Any of several types of social organization in which the individual is seen as being subordinate to a social collectivity such as a state, a nation, a race, or a social class. Collectivism may be contrasted with individualism, in which the rights and interests of the individual are emphasized". http://www.britannica.com/EBchecked/topic/125584/collectivism

Command Economy Otherwise called Communist state is an economic system where the means of production is centralized or publicly owned or controlled. "A system where the government, rather than the free market, determines what goods should be produced, how much should be produced and the price at which the goods will be offered for sale". http://www.investopedia.com/terms/c/command-economy.asp

Cost-Push Inflation A type of inflation caused by substantial increases in the cost of goods or services where no suitable alternative is available or due to an increase in wages or cost of raw materials

Gold Standard Era Gold standard was an understanding among committed countries to fix the exchange rate of their local currencies against a specified amount of gold. The period between 1870 and 1914 when this system was in place is referred to as the Gold Standard Era. The classical Gold standard era is between 1880 and 1914.

The Greenspan Put refers to the monetary policy approach that Alan Greenspan, the former chairman of the United States Federal Reserve Board, and other Fed members exercised from late 1987 to 2000. The term 'Put' refers to a put option, in which the buyer of the put acquires the right to sell an asset at a particular price to a counterparty; it can be exercised if prices decline below that price. http://en.wikipedia.org/wiki/Greenspan_put

Gross Domestic Product (GDP) The total market value of all the finished goods and services produced in a country in a given year or a specific time period. It is equal to all private and public consumption, government spending, investments and exports less imports that occur within a defined territory. GDP is usually reported on an annual basis

Hurdle Rates The rate of return that a fund manager must beat before collecting incentive fees. It is the minimum rate of return on investment required by a management or investor to compensate for a risk

Individualism The social theory or principle that supports the freedom of individual over collective or state dominion. "Political and social philosophy that emphasizes the moral worth of the individual. Although the concept of an individual may seem straightforward, there are many ways of understanding it, both in theory and in practice. The term *individualism* itself, and its equivalents in other languages, dates—like socialism and other *isms*—from the 19th century" http://www.britannica.com/EBchecked/topic/286303/individualism

Monetary Contraction The monetary policy that reduces the size of the money circulated in an economy through tax increases as corrective measures. This macroeconomic tool is used by the central bank to reduce the money in circulation usually to fight inflation or reduce government spending

Renminbi (RMD) Is the official currency of the People Republic of China. It is usually abbreviated as RMD

Smith's Principle of the Mercantile System A model of political and economic system where money is regarded as the store of wealth and the ultimate goal of the state is the accumulation of precious metals through the exportation of largest possible quantity of product and importing as little as possible thus creating a favourable balance of trade. The aim is to enhance state power at the expense of a rival state.

Soft Law (Loose Financial Policies) Soft laws are regulations that are not strictly binding in nature or completely lacking in legal significance. Soft laws are directives, guidelines, policy declarations or codes of conduct which set standards of conduct. They cannot be directly enforceable.

Tobin's Q' Theory (Ratio, of Investment) A measure of firm asset in relation to a firm's market value. It is a ratio of price to replacement cost in relation to a firm's market value. In this economic theory of investment behaviour the 'q' represents the ratio of the market value of a firm's existing shares to the replacement cost of a firm's physical assets

Zero-Sum Game Refers to a situation where one person's gain is equivalent to the other person's loss. The implication is that the net change in wealth or benefit is constant. The balancing of the gains of one participant to reduce to zero the gains of the other participants.

BIBLIOGRAPHY

Adair, A. et al. (2009). Global Financial Crisis: Impact on Property Markets in the UK and Ireland: http://news.ulster.ac.uk/podcasts/ReiGlobalCrisis.pdf, accessed 30 July 2010.

Adam, S (2010). http://web.ebscohost.com.ezproxy.wales.ac.uk:2048/ehost/detail?vid=27&hid=110&sid=9fca6a59-ea6a-4ebc-9a3a-3d71a05bd288%40sessionmgr115&bdata=JnNpdGU9ZWhvc3QtbGl2ZSZzY29wZT1zaXRl#db=bth&AN=48125985, accessed 25 July 2011.

Albrecht, A (2010). Lessons to Be Learnt from the Consumer Credit Crunch: http://www.fondation-droitcontinental.org/upload/docs/application/pdf/2010-08/albrecht_lessons_to_be_learnt_from_the_consumer_credit_crunch.pdf, accessed 5 August 2011.

Asensio, A. and D. Lang (2010). The Financial Crisis: Its Economic Consequences: http://web.ebscohost.com.ezproxy.wales.ac.uk:2048/ehost/pdfviewer/pdfviewer?sid=a1a8aa3b-38b7-4f3d-9cd4-0cbac30205a6%40sessionmgr115&vid=4&hid=107, accessed 3 July 2011.

BBC News (2011). 'Barack Obama Presses for Middle East Reform': http://www.bbc.co.uk/news/world-us-canada-13450481, accessed 10 August 2011.

BBC News (2011). 'UK Recession "Worst Since 1930s"': http://news.bbc.co.uk/2/hi/business/8034879.stm, accessed 10 May 2011.

Bernanke, BS (2009). Speech delivered by chairman Bernanke: 'Four Questions about the Financial Crisis': http://www.federalreserve.gov/

newsevents/speech/bernanke20090414a.htm#pagetop, accessed 15 August 2011.

Birol, F (2009). 'The Impact of the Crisis on Energy Industry': http://www.iea.org/ebc/files/impact.pdf, accessed 10 May 2011.

Blanchard, O (2000). *Macroeconomics,* 2nd ed., New Jersey: Practice Hall.

Bogle, JC (2008). 'Black Monday and Black Swans': http://web.ebscohost.com.ezproxy.wales.ac.uk:2048/ehost/detail?vid=3&hid=110&sid=cd3370d0-5946-44fb-8dcd-887bb6245b0b%40sessionmgr114&bdata=JnNpdGU9ZWhvc3QtbGl2ZSZzY29wZT1zaXRl#db=bth&AN=31597082, accessed 12 August 2011.

Borchardt, R. and J. Cooper (2009). 'Picking up the Pieces': http://web.ebscohost.com.ezproxy.wales.ac.uk:2048/ehost/detail?vid=9&hid=106&sid=139cbe37-a30b-4326-acf7-07481ee5bebb%40sessionmgr112&bdata=JnNpdGU9ZWhvc3QtbGl2ZSZzY29wZT1zaXRl, accessed 15 August 2011.

Brabant, M (2010). 'Three Dead as Greece Protest Turns Violent': http://news.bbc.co.uk/2/hi/8661385.stm, accessed 10 August 2011.

Brasoveanu, IV and LO Brasoveanu (2011). 'Effects of the Current Economic Crisis on the Fiscal Variables in EU Countries': http://web.ebscohost.com.ezproxy.wales.ac.uk:2048/ehost/detail?vid=3&hid=108&sid=dacdda38-1089-441f-86d4-af141369cf5e%40sessionmgr111&bdata=JnNpdGU9ZWhvc3QtbGl2ZSZzY29wZT1zaXRl#db=bth&AN=59149556, accessed 25 June 2011.

Bratton, WW (2002). 'Enron and the Dark Side of Shareholder Value': http://papers.ssrn.com/sol3/papers.cfm?abstract_id=301475, accessed 30 October 2011.

Browning, ES (2007). 'Exorcising Ghosts of October Past': http://online.wsj.com/article/SB119239926667758592.html?mod=mkts_main_news_hs_h, accessed 12 August 2011,

Burry, M (2011). Missteps to Mayhem: http://www.vanderbilt.edu/magazines/vanderbilt-magazine/2011/09/missteps-to-mayhem/, accessed 29 October 2011.

Businessweek (2004) How Parmalat Went Sour: http://www.businessweek.com/magazine/content/04_02/b3865053_mz054.htm, accessed 28 July 2011.

Calmes, J. and C. Hulse (2011). 'Moody's Warns of Downgrade for US Credit': http://www.nytimes.com/2011/06/03/us/politics/03congress.html?_r=1&hp, accessed 25 June 2011.

'Canadian CP Market Reaches Broad Agreement' (2008): http://web.ebscohost.com.ezproxy.wales.ac.uk:2048/ehost/detail?vid=3&hid=112&sid=34f0703b-152f-4c1d-a49f-6b17378cfbcc%40sessionmgr111&bdata=JnNpdGU9ZWhvc3QtbGl2ZSZzY29wZT1zaXRl#db=bth&AN=62242085, accessed 29 July 2011.

Chandra, S (2010). 'Recession in US Was Even More Than Estimated': http://www.bloomberg.com/news/2010-07-30/recession-in-america-was-even-worse-than-estimated-revisions-to-data-show.html, accessed 20 October 2011.

'Citi Faces Belgian Lehman – Linked Suits' (2009): http://web.ebscohost.com.ezproxy.wales.ac.uk:2048/ehost/detail?vid=3&hid=107&sid=b407c86c-0586-4ba6-8201-1905f455e4f2%40sessionmgr104&bdata=JnNpdGU9ZWhvc3QtbGl2ZSZzY29wZT1zaXRl#db=bth&AN=55121830 accessed 5 August 2011)

Damary R. 'The Online MBA – Investment Management', Unpublished working paper presented at Robert Kennedy College, 3 September 2010.

Danielsen, BR and SM Sorescu (2001). 'Why Do Option Introduction Depress Market: http://web.ebscohost.com.ezproxy.wales.ac.uk:2048/ehost/detail?vid=3&hid=110&sid=cd3370d0-5946-44fb-8dcd-887bb6245b0b%40sessionmgr114&bdata=JnNpdGU9ZWhvc3QtbGl2ZSZzY29wZT1zaXRl#db=bth&AN=6038932, accessed 11 August 2011.

Deane, A (2005). Capitalism versus Socialism: http://www.idebate.org/debatabase/topic_details.php?topicID=400, accessed 29 August 2011)

Diana, B. and PC Madalina (2008). 'Is Creative Accounting a Form of Manipulation?' http://steconomice.uoradea.ro/anale/volume/2008/v3-finances-banks-accountancy/172.pdf, accessed 30 October 2011.

'Europe's Most Earnest Protesters'. *The Economist* (2011), http://web.ebscohost.com.ezproxy.wales.ac.uk:2048/ehost/resultsadvanced?sid=9fca6a59-ea6a-4ebc-9a3a-3d71a05bd288%40sessionmgr115&vid=25&hid=110&bquery=(the+indignant+&quot%3bin&quot%3b+spain)&bdata=JmRiPWJ0aCZjbGkwPUZUJmNsdjA9WSZ0eXBlPTAmc2l0ZT1laG9zdC1saXZlJnNjb3BlPXNpdGU%3d, accessed 1 August 2011.

Edey, M (2009). 'Global Financial Crisis and its Effects': http://web.ebscohost.com.ezproxy.wales.ac.uk:2048/ehost/detail?vid=3&hid=110&sid=0174acaa-c401-457d-9e9b-9be4509758d3%40sessionmgr114&bdata=JnNpdGU9ZWhvc3QtbGl2ZSZzY29wZT1zaXRl#db=bth&AN=48044802, accessed 10 august 2010.

Elan, E (2009). 'Economy Rocks New York City Landmarks': http://web.ebscohost.com.ezproxy.wales.ac.uk:2048/ehost/pdfviewer/pdfviewer?sid=a4259fb6-a284-4dc6-9d77-f7b91fb6c9ad%40sessionmgr112&vid=4&hid=111, accessed 30 July 2010.

Elliot, B. and J. Elliot (2004). *Financial Accounting and Reporting*, 4th ed., London: Prentice Hall.

Fitzpatrick, L (2010). New York: http://web.ebscohost.com.ezproxy.wales.ac.uk:2048/ehost/detail?sid=9fca6a59-ea6a-4ebc-9a3a-3d71a05bd288%40sessionmgr115&vid=7&hid=110&bdata=JnNpdGU9ZWhvc3QtbGl2ZSZzY29wZT1zaXRl#db=bth&AN=48125984, accessed 27 July 2011.

Fisher, I (1906). *The Nature of Capital and Income*, 1st ed., New York: Macmillan.

Forden, SG (2008). 'Parmalat's Tanzi Sentenced to 10 years in Milan Trial': http://www.bloomberg.com/apps/news?pid=newsarchive&sid=alrsQE4_kBPU&refer=home, accessed 3 August 2011.

Franklin, A (2010). 'An Overview of the Crisis: Causes, Consequences, and Solutions': http://web.ebscohost.com.ezproxy.wales.ac.uk:2048/ehost/detail?vid=5&hid=119&sid=f239380f-e300-49a7-b474-31e5bd268f68%40sessionmgr112&bdata=JnNpdGU9ZWhvc3QtbGl2ZSZzY29wZT1zaXRl#db=bth&AN=48328782, accessed 3 August 2010.

Gocen, CA (2010). 'Corporate Governance Internal Audit and Independent Audit: Parmalat Case': http://web.ebscohost.com.ezproxy.wales.ac.uk:2048/ehost/detail?vid=3&hid=107&sid=b407c86c-0586-4ba6-8201-1905f455e4f2%40sessionmgr104&bdata=JnNpdGU9ZWhvc3QtbGl2ZSZzY29wZT1zaXRl#db=bth&AN=51545597, accessed 6 August 2011.

Goldberg, LS (2006). 'Exchange Rates and Foreign Direct Investment': http://www.newyorkfed.org/research/economists/goldberg/ERandFDIArticleGoldberg.pdf, accessed 1 November 2011.

Gruenewald, SN (2010). 'Financial Crisis Containment and its Implications for Institutional and Legal Reform': http://web.ebscohost.com.ezproxy.wales.ac.uk:2048/ehost/detail?vid=3&hid=112&sid=1f31b8ad-5ae4-417a-bf87-8d9248502c8c%40sessionmgr112&bdata=JnNpdGU9ZWhvc3QtbGl2ZSZzY29wZT1zaXRl#db=bth&AN=55773849, accessed 28 July 2011.

Guardian, The (2003). Parmalat Scandal Special report: http://www.guardian.co.uk/parmalat/0,14141,1114024,00.html, accessed 28 July 2011.

Guardian, The (2004). Milking the Company: http://www.guardian.co.uk/world/2004/jan/01/italy.parmalat, accessed 2nd August 2011.

Guide to Social Security Law (2011). http://www.fahcsia.gov.au/guides_acts/ssg/ssguide-4/ssguide-4.6/ssguide-4.6.5/ssguide-4.6.5.110.html#, accessed 1 July 2011.

Hawkes, A (2011). 'Italy Downgrade Adds to Eurozone Contagion Fear': http://www.guardian.co.uk/business/2011/sep/20/italy-downgrade-eurozone-contagion-fear, accessed 25 September 2011.

Hewitt, JR (2010). 'The Unemployment Blues': http://web.ebscohost.com.ezproxy.wales.ac.uk:2048/ehost/pdfviewer/pdfviewer?sid=cce5ed37-5ec5-402b-80a2-c12f3c7bc5ce%40sessionmgr115&vid=11&hid=127, accessed 28 July 2010.

Hill, CWL (2009). *International Business*, 7th ed., New York McGraw-Hill/Irwin.

Italian Stock exchange (2011). Debt Figure: http://www.borsaitaliana.it/notizie/speciali/obbligazioni/tipologie-di-obbligazioni/bot-btp-ctz-debito-italiano-sul-mercato/il-debito-italiano-sul-mercato.htm, accessed 8 August 2011.

Jackson, JK (2010). The Financial Crisis: Impact and Response by the EU: http://web.ebscohost.com.ezproxy.wales.ac.uk:2048/ehost/detail?vid=8&hid=127&sid=cce5ed37-5ec5-402b-80a2-c12f3c7bc5ce%40sessionmgr115&bdata=JnNpdGU9ZWhvc3QtbGl2ZSZzY29wZT1zaXRl#db=bth&AN=59923648, accessed 28 July 2010.

Keynes, JM (1936). *The General Theory of Employment. Interest and Money*, 1st ed., Cambridge: Macmillan.

Khanna, G. et al. (2009). 'Fewer Jobs or Smaller Paycheques': http://ftp.iza.org/dp5956.pdf, accessed 20 July 2011.

Koons, C (2011). 'Australia Investors Confidence at Lowest Level Since 2009': http://online.wsj.com/article/SB10001424053111904537404576551331735923152.html?mod=rss_economy, accessed 25 November 2011.

Kwan, S (2009). 'Behaviour of Libor in the Current Financial Crisis': http://www.frbsf.org/publications/economics/letter/2009/el2009-04.html, accessed 13 August 2011.

Lahart, J (2007). 'Egg Cracks Differ in Housing Finance Shell': http://online.wsj.com/article/SB119845906460548071.html?mod=googlenews_wsj, accessed 28 October 2011.

_____. (2009). 'Mr Rajan was Unpopular but (Prescient) at Greenspan Party': http://online.wsj.com/article/SB123086154114948151.html, accessed 5 August 2011.

Laudon, KC and JP Laudon (2002). *Management Information System*, 7th ed., New Jersey: Prentice.

Levisohn, B (2009). Pound Play: http://web.ebscohost.com.ezproxy.wales.ac.uk:2048/ehost/detail?vid=12&hid=127&sid=cce5ed37-5ec5-402b-80a2-c12f3c7bc5ce%40sessionmgr115&bdata=JnNpdGU9ZWhvc3QtbGl2ZSZzY29wZT1zaXRl#db=bth&AN=36332661, accessed 29 July 2010.

Mankiw GN (2000). *Macroeconomics*, 4th ed. New York: Worth Publishers.

_____ (2007). *Principles of Economics*, 4th ed. Thomson South Western: Harvard University.

'Market Abuse, Summaries of EU Legislation' (2003): http://europa.eu/legislation_summaries/internal_market/single_market_services/financial_services_transactions_in_securities/l24035_en.htm, accessed 10 August 2011.

Markowitz, HM (1959). *Portfolio Selection*, 1st ed., New York: John Willy & son.

McLaney, E. and P. Atrill (2008). *Accounting: an Introduction*, 4th ed., Harlow: Prentice Hall.

Mullins, LJ (2002). *Management and Organizational Behaviour*, 6th ed., Harlow: Prentice.

Nordt, John C., et al. (2012). 'As Medicare Costs Rise, Reimbursements Drop': http://www.quebecoislibre.org/05/050915-11.htm, accessed 10 April 2013.

Novembre, V (2009). 'The Bargaining Process as a Variable to Explain Implementation Choices of Soft Law: the Basel Case Study', *Journal of Banking Regulation* (2009) 10, 128–152. doi:10.1057/jbr.2008.23.

Oranika, P (2011). 'Should Hedge Funds Be Regulated?' http://www.hedgeco.net/hedge-fund-regulations.htm, accessed 4 August 2011.

Perry, B (2011). 'Credit Crisis: Market Effects': http://www.investopedia.com/university/credit-crisis/credit-crisis7.asp#axzz1gKhBfQ22, accessed 24 July 2011.

Pindyck, RS (1991). Irreversibility, Uncertainty and Investment: http://scholar.google.com/scholar?q=pindyck+1991+irreversibility+uncertainty+and+investment&hl=en&as_sdt=0&as_vis=1&oi=scholart, accessed 20 September 2011.

Puiu, S (2009). 'The Effects of the Economic and Financial Crisis': http://web.ebscohost.com.ezproxy.wales.ac.uk:2048/ehost/pdfviewer/pdfviewer?sid=139cbe37-a30b-4326-acf7-07481ee5bebb%40sessionmgr112&vid=7&hid=106, accessed 13 August 2011.

Rajan, RG (2005). 'Has Financial Development Made the World Riskier?': http://www.nber.org/papers/w1172, accessed 8 August 2011.

Robbins, SP (2005). *Organizational Behaviour*, 11th ed., New Jersey: Prentice Hall.

Roberts, R. et al. (2004). 'Spilt Milk: Parmalat and Sarbanes-Oxley Internal Control Reporting': http://web.ebscohost.com.ezproxy.wales.ac.uk:2048/ehost/pdfviewer/pdfviewer?sid=b407c86c-0586-4ba6-8201-1905f455e4f2%40sessionmgr104&vid=4&hid=107, accessed 5 August 2011.

Romer CD and DH Romer (2007). 'The Macroeconomic Effects of Tax Changes': http://elsa.berkeley.edu/~cromer/RomerDraft307.pdf, accessed 30 October 2011.

Salahuddin, M. and R. Islam (2008). 'Factor Affecting Investment in Developing Countries': http://web.ebscohost.com.ezproxy.wales.ac.uk:2048/ehost/results?sid=cce5ed37-5ec5-402b-80a2-c12f3c7bc5ce%40sessionmgr115&vid=2&hid=127&bquery=(factors+affecting+investment+&quot%3bIN&quot%3b)&bdata=JmRiPWJ0aCZjbGkwPUZUJmNsdjA9WSZ0eXBlPTAmc2l0ZT1laG9zdC1saXZlJnNjb3BlPXNpdGU%3d, accessed 28 July 2011.

Samuelson, RJ (2007). 'China's Wrong Turn on Trade': http://www.thedailybeast.com/newsweek/2007/05/14/china-s-wrong-turn-on-trade.html, accessed 28 October 2011.

Schiff, D (1993). *The Dangers of Creative Accounting Worth* (March): 92-94.

Sendanyoye, J (2009). 'Impact of the Financial Crisis on Finance Sector Workers': http://www.ilo.org/wcmsp5/groups/public/@dgreports/@dcomm/documents/meetingdocument/wcms_103263.pdf, accessed 20 October 2011.

Sexton, RL (2008). *Exploring Economics*, 4th ed., South Western: Thomson Learning.

Spiegel Online (2009). 'Burned by Lehman Securities: German Bank Admits Giving Wrong Advise to Investors': http://www.spiegel.de/international/business/0,1518,621599,00.html, accessed 20 August 2011.

State Aid Rules (1997). 'Article 87': http://www.reckon.co.uk/open/Article_87, accessed 21st August 2011.

Stoukas, T (2011). 'Austerity Calling: Portraits of the New Greece': http://web.ebscohost.com.ezproxy.wales.ac.uk:2048/ehost/pdfviewer/pdfviewer?sid=f239380f-e300-49a7-b474-31e5bd268f68%40sessionmgr112&vid=4&hid=119, accessed 1 August 2011.

Alexander, et al. (2008). The State of the Nation Housing Report: http://www.jchs.harvard.edu/publications/markets/son2008/son2008.pdf, accessed 10 August 2011.

United States Census Bureau (2011). http://www.census.gov/, accessed 31 July 2011.

United States Commerce Department (2011). 'Effects of the Crisis on the US': http://www.commerce.gov/, accessed 10 May 2011.

United States Treasury (2011) Debt Figure: http://www.treasurydirect.gov/govt/reports/pd/pd_debtposactrpt_1105.pdf, accessed 25 May 2011.

'What Have We Become?' *The Economist* (2011), http://web.ebscohost.com.ezproxy.wales.ac.uk:2048/ehost/detail?sid=f239380f-e300-49a7-

b474-31e5bd268f68%40sessionmgr112&vid=4&hid=119&bdata=JnNp dGU9ZWhvc3QtbGl2ZSZzY29wZT1zaXRl#db=bth&AN=64302262, accessed 2 August 2011.

Weber, T (2008). 'Who's Afraid of the Sovereign Wealth Fund?' http://news.bbc.co.uk/2/hi/business/7207715.stm, accessed 15 September 2011.

Younkins, EW (2005). Capitalism and commerce: http://www.quebecoislibre.org/05/050915-11.htm.

www.ingramcontent.com/pod-product-compliance
Lightning Source LLC
Chambersburg PA
CBHW030854180526
45163CB00004B/1573